Table Of Contents:

Introduction: The Real Cost of Overspending 4

1. The Leaking Wallet: How Your Money Drains Away......... 6
2. Uncovering the Invisible Hand of Consumerism..............14
3. Facing the Truth: Your Spending Audit........................... 21
4. The Power of No: Reclaiming Control Over Your Wallet.... 29
5. Mastering Minimalism: Spending With Purpose............... 35
6. Smart Cuts: Where to Trim Without Pain......................... 40
7. Beating Subscription Fatigue.. 45
8: Building a Fortress of Savings.. 50
9: Building a Fortress of Savings.. 56
10: Automating Your Way to Wealth................................... 63
11: Celebrating Small Wins.. 70
12: Investing in Yourself: The Best Return on Investment..... 77
13: Turning Expenses Into Opportunities 84
14: The Debt Detox: Clearing the Path to Freedom.............. 90
15: Creating a Future-Proof Budget.................................... 97
16: The Emotional Rewards of Saving Smarter................... 104
17: From Consumer to Creator: Redefining Success.......... 111

18: Empowering Others: Sharing the Wealth Mindset……….. 118

19: Conclusion - Your New Financial Life ..……..…….…… 125

1. Introduction: The Real Cost of Overspending

Why Your Finances Feel Out of Control

- The Invisible Drain: Explore how money seems to vanish without explanation, leaving you wondering, Where did it all go? Hidden costs like automatic renewals, small daily purchases, and lifestyle inflation contribute to the slow bleed of your wallet.

- Emotional Spending: Discuss the psychological triggers behind overspending—stress relief, boredom, or seeking validation. Highlight how these habits compound financial instability while offering only temporary satisfaction.

- The Shame Spiral: Unpack the cycle of guilt and regret that follows overspending, leading many to avoid confronting their finances altogether. Address how this avoidance can worsen the problem.

- The External Pressures: Explain how societal expectations, marketing, and social media amplify the need to spend. The "highlight reel" culture fuels a desire to keep up, often at the expense of financial well-being.

A New Approach to Saving Without Sacrifice

- Rethinking Saving: Reframe saving as a form of empowerment rather than deprivation. Discuss the emotional and psychological benefits of taking control of your finances, such as reduced stress and increased confidence.

- Focusing on Priorities: Introduce the concept of purposeful spending—channeling your money toward what genuinely aligns with your values and goals, rather than fleeting desires.

- Sustainable Habits: Emphasize the importance of small, consistent changes that lead to lasting results. Instead of drastic budgeting, focus on realistic adjustments that fit seamlessly into your lifestyle.

- A Vision for Financial Freedom: Paint a vivid picture of what life looks like when you master your finances—freedom from paycheck-to-paycheck living, the ability to seize opportunities, and the peace of knowing you're prepared for life's uncertainties.

- An Invitation to Transform: Encourage readers to commit to the journey ahead, reassuring them that this ebook will provide the tools, mindset shifts, and strategies needed to cut costs and save smarter without feeling restricted.

chapter 1: "The Leaking Wallet: How Your Money Drains Away."

Part 1: Understanding the Problem

Chapter 1: The Leaking Wallet: How Your Money Drains Away

Section 1: The Emotional Toll of Financial Drains

Jenna's daily coffee habit started as a simple indulgence, a small way to treat herself and set a positive tone for her mornings. But as the weeks turned into months, the $6 lattes quietly accumulated, adding up to a staggering $180 a month—nearly $2,200 a year. The realization struck her like a tidal wave, washing over her with regret and self-reproach. That money could have funded a gym membership to improve her health or paid for a weekend getaway to recharge her spirit. Instead, it was gone, spent on a fleeting pleasure she barely remembered enjoying. Jenna felt frustrated and wasteful, questioning how something so small could derail her larger goals.

Similarly, Marcus faced a sobering reality when he reviewed his subscription expenses. The five streaming services he'd signed up for in the name of variety had become silent financial drains. Three of them, which he rarely used, were costing him $45 a month—over $500 annually. The realization felt like a slap, intensified by the thought of how easily he could have redirected that money toward something meaningful. These financial leaks, though seemingly minor, served as stark reminders of the emotional toll of unchecked spending. The sting of guilt and frustration they felt underscores a critical lesson: recognizing and addressing these patterns is essential to regaining control and aligning spending with purpose.

Example 1: The Daily Coffee Run

- **Scenario:** Every morning, Jenna stops at a trendy coffee shop and spends $6 on a latte. At first, it feels like a harmless treat, a reward for starting the day early. But as the weeks go by, Jenna realizes she's spending nearly $180 a month on coffee—enough to pay for a gym membership or save toward a weekend getaway.

- **Emotional Impact:** When Jenna calculates the annual total, the realization hits like a wave of regret. She feels guilty, wasteful, and frustrated with herself for prioritizing fleeting pleasures over meaningful goals.

Example 2: Streaming Overload

- **Scenario:** Marcus subscribes to five different streaming services, each costing around $15 a month. He hardly uses three of them but keeps them "just in case." After a year, he calculates that he's spent over $500 on unused entertainment.

- **Emotional Impact:** Marcus feels the sharp sting of wasted money, compounded by the nagging thought that he didn't even notice the drain until now.

Lesson: These examples reveal the emotional burden of financial drains —not just the monetary loss but the guilt and regret that accompany it. Recognizing these patterns is the first step toward taking control.

Section 2: Impulse Buys, Forgotten Subscriptions, and Lifestyle Inflation

Sarah and Jamal's experiences highlight the emotional traps of impulse shopping and lifestyle inflation, revealing how easily financial decisions can spiral into regret. For Sarah, the allure of a social media flash sale delivers a fleeting rush of dopamine, a momentary thrill that turns sour when she opens her package to find items she doesn't even like. Each purchase leaves her feeling more frustrated, her closet cluttered with clothes that symbolize wasted money and unmet expectations. Meanwhile, Jamal's promotion, meant to signify progress, becomes a source of stress as his upgraded lifestyle consumes his new paycheck. The luxurious amenities he once celebrated now feel like anchors, weighing down his financial goals. Both scenarios illustrate how emotional triggers like boredom, stress, or the desire to reward oneself can lead to decisions that undermine long-term stability. Recognizing these patterns is crucial; only by addressing the emotions driving these habits can individuals like Sarah and Jamal reclaim control and realign their spending with their true priorities.

Example 1: Impulse Shopping Online

- **Scenario:** Sarah scrolls through social media and sees a flash sale for clothes. The dopamine hit from snagging a deal is instant, but a week later, the package arrives, and she realizes she doesn't even like the items. Over a year, these impulse purchases add up to hundreds of dollars wasted.

- **Emotional Impact:** Sarah feels ashamed for falling into the trap repeatedly, knowing she's cluttered her closet and depleted her bank account for things she didn't truly want.

Example 2: Lifestyle Inflation After a Raise

- **Scenario:** After earning a promotion, Jamal moves into a luxury apartment with amenities he barely uses. While his new lifestyle feels good initially, his paycheck disappears faster than before, leaving him stressed about paying bills.

- **Emotional Impact:** The realization that his new income hasn't improved his financial stability feels crushing. Jamal starts to wonder if the trade-off was worth it.

Lesson: Impulse buys and lifestyle inflation often stem from emotional triggers like boredom, stress, or the desire to celebrate. Identifying these triggers can help you make smarter spending decisions.

Section 3: Recognizing Your Spending Triggers

Andrea and Tyler illustrate how emotional spending can create a relentless cycle of regret and financial instability. For Andrea, the rush of a shopping spree after a tough day offers fleeting comfort, a momentary balm for her stress. But when the credit card bill arrives, the reality of her impulsive decisions weighs heavy, trapping her in a loop of guilt and anxiety. Similarly, Tyler's desire to keep up with his friends' glamorous lives on social media drives him to book an unaffordable vacation, leaving him burdened by debt and resentment. Both scenarios highlight the emotional triggers—stress, peer pressure, and the need for validation—that fuel reckless spending. By recognizing these patterns, Andrea and Tyler can begin to break free, replacing temporary fixes with healthier coping mechanisms and a stronger focus on financial well-being.

Example 1: Emotional Spending After a Hard Day

- **Scenario:** After a stressful workday, Andrea rewards herself with a shopping spree, rationalizing that she "deserves it." She buys items she doesn't need, only to feel regret the next day when the credit card bill arrives.

- **Emotional Impact:** Andrea feels trapped in a cycle of emotional spending, where the short-term relief is outweighed by long-term financial anxiety.

Example 2: Peer Pressure and Social Media Influence

- **Scenario:** Tyler sees his friends post pictures of expensive vacations online. Feeling left out, he books a last-minute trip he can't afford just to keep up. The vacation is enjoyable, but the debt it leaves him with causes sleepless nights.

- **Emotional Impact:** Tyler feels resentful—not just of the debt but of the societal pressure to appear successful.

Lesson: By identifying emotional spending triggers—stress, social influence, or self-reward—you can build awareness and develop healthier ways to cope.

Section 4: Understanding Financial Blind Spots

Danielle and Alex's experiences highlight the hidden costs of financial neglect and the emotional toll they can take. Danielle's avoidance of her bank statements left her blind to recurring subscription charges she believed were canceled. The accumulating small expenses, once unnoticed, snowballed into a significant financial burden, leaving her feeling careless and out of control. Similarly, Alex's reliance on food delivery apps for convenience masked the mounting costs of fees and tips, which quietly drained over $200 from his monthly budget. When he finally took stock, the frustration of seeing how these choices derailed his financial goals was palpable. These stories underscore the importance of actively engaging with your finances—reviewing statements and questioning spending habits can shine a light on hidden drains, empowering you to regain control and align your spending with your goals.Example 1: Ignoring Bank Statements

- **Scenario:** Danielle avoids looking at her bank statements because it feels overwhelming. As a result, she doesn't realize she's being charged for a subscription she thought she canceled months ago. Over time, these small charges amount to hundreds of dollars.

- **Emotional Impact:** The shock of discovering these overlooked expenses makes Danielle feel careless and out of control.

Example 2: Overpaying for Convenience

- **Scenario:** Alex uses a food delivery app daily instead of cooking or grocery shopping. While it saves time, the delivery fees and tips add up to over $200 a month, which he hadn't budgeted for.

- **Emotional Impact:** Alex feels frustrated when he realizes his convenience habit has derailed his financial goals.

Lesson: Ignoring financial details creates blind spots that lead to unnecessary expenses. Regularly reviewing accounts and questioning convenience spending can reveal hidden drains.

Section 5: The Compounding Effect of Small Expenses

Rashad and Karen's experiences highlight how seemingly small financial decisions can quietly erode financial stability. Rashad's $5 here and there on snacks, parking meters, and vending machines felt insignificant in the moment, but the cumulative $150 monthly expense was a wake-up call. It wasn't the occasional treat but the untracked pattern that snowballed into a costly habit. Similarly, Karen's enthusiasm for bulk sales seemed like smart shopping, but over time, her home filled with unused items, and her intentions to save backfired as products expired, leaving her feeling wasteful and burdened by clutter. Both scenarios underline the importance of mindfulness in spending. When small decisions are made without awareness, they can quietly drain resources and sabotage financial goals. Learning to pause, track, and question everyday choices empowers individuals to prevent these financial leaks and channel their money toward more meaningful priorities.

Example 1: The $5 Rule

- **Scenario:** Rashad often spends $5 here and there—on vending machines, parking meters, and snacks. Individually, these expenses seem minor, but over a month, they total over $150.

- **Emotional Impact:** Rashad is shocked to see how small, daily choices snowballed into a significant financial leak.

Example 2: Buying "Affordable" Items in Bulk

- **Scenario:** Karen loves sales and buys items in bulk because they're "affordable." However, she ends up with more than she can use, and many items expire or go unused. The waste leaves her feeling foolish and wasteful.

- **Emotional Impact:** Karen realizes her attempts to save money have backfired, leaving her with clutter and financial regret.

Lesson: Small expenses, when left unchecked, can have a significant impact over time. Awareness and mindfulness are essential to prevent these financial leaks.

Section 6: Building Awareness Through Reflection

Lisa had always felt like her paycheck disappeared faster than she could track, so she decided to start a spending journal, meticulously logging every dollar she spent for 30 days. At first, the process was tedious and even uncomfortable, as it forced her to confront the sheer volume of unnecessary purchases—her frequent dining out, the quick coffee stops, and the seemingly harmless $10 purchases that added up alarmingly fast. By the end of the month, she stared at her journal with a mix of emotions: embarrassment over how much she had spent on non-essentials but also a newfound sense of empowerment. For the first time, she could see exactly where her money was going and identify patterns she hadn't noticed before. With this clarity, Lisa felt motivated to make intentional changes, armed with the knowledge that her finances were no longer a mystery, but something she could control. Her experience underscores a vital truth: reflecting on spending habits is the key to breaking the cycle and building financial confidence.

Example 1: The Spending Journal

- **Scenario:** Lisa starts tracking every expense in a journal for 30 days. Seeing her habits on paper helps her recognize patterns, like frequent dining out, that she hadn't noticed before.

- **Emotional Impact:** Lisa feels a mix of embarrassment and empowerment—embarrassed by her spending but empowered to take action.

Example 2: Monthly Financial Review
- **Scenario:** Chris sets aside an hour each month to review his bank and credit card statements. During his first review, he finds duplicate charges and forgotten subscriptions, saving him over $100 immediately.

- **Emotional Impact:** Chris feels relieved and motivated to continue the habit, knowing it gives him control over his finances.

Lesson: Reflecting on your spending habits regularly is a powerful tool for identifying problems and staying accountable.

Summary of Lessons Learned

- Awareness Is Key: Recognizing financial drains and spending triggers is the first step toward control.
- Emotions Drive Spending: Impulse buys, lifestyle inflation, and convenience spending often stem from emotional triggers like stress or the desire for social validation.
- Small Leaks Matter: Even minor, daily expenses can compound into significant financial drains.
- Reflection Changes Behavior: Tools like spending journals and monthly reviews empower you to identify and correct spending patterns.

chapter 2: "Uncovering the Invisible Hand of Consumerism."

Chapter 2. Uncovering the Invisible Hand of Consumerism

Part 1: How Marketing Exploits Your Emotions

Marketing is a master of manipulation, using emotional triggers to drive impulsive decisions that often leave us with buyer's remorse. Take the classic "Limited Time Only" campaign—a scarcity tactic designed to create a false sense of urgency. When a luxury brand releases a "seasonal collection," it sparks FOMO (fear of missing out), making you feel as though this fleeting opportunity must be seized. Similarly, emotionally charged advertisements, like a family smiling on a sunlit beach with the tagline "Because they're worth it," pull at your heartstrings, equating spending with love and care. These strategies exploit deeply human desires for belonging, love, and security, pushing you to buy things that may not align with your actual needs or values. The key to breaking free is awareness: recognize the manufactured urgency and emotional bait, and pause to ask yourself if the purchase genuinely adds value to your life—or if it's just a clever trick to open your wallet.

- **Example 1: The Scarcity Trap**
    - Marketing campaigns often use phrases like "Limited Time Only" or "Last Chance" to create a false sense of urgency. Imagine a luxury brand releasing a "seasonal collection" and implying exclusivity. Consumers feel compelled to act quickly, driven by the fear of missing out (FOMO), even if the purchase doesn't align with their real needs.

    - **Lesson:** Recognize when urgency is being manufactured. Ask yourself: Do I really need this right now, or am I being pressured by a clever marketing tactic?

- **Example 2: Emotional Targeting in Advertising**
    - Consider an advertisement featuring a family enjoying a lavish holiday, with the tagline, "Because they're worth it." The emotional undertone is clear: if you care about your loved ones, you'll spend money to create such moments. This tactic preys on feelings of guilt or inadequacy to drive purchases.

    - **Lesson:** Acknowledge the emotional triggers in marketing. Before purchasing, ask: Am I buying this to fulfill an emotional void or because it truly adds value to my life?

Part 2: The Psychology Behind "Treat Yourself" Culture

The "treat yourself" culture taps into our desire for instant gratification, often leading to financial decisions driven by emotion rather than intention. Consider the rush of excitement that comes with retail therapy—a designer handbag purchased after a stressful day might provide a fleeting sense of triumph, but that high fades quickly, leaving behind the weight of guilt when the bill arrives. Similarly, the justification spiral plays into the narrative of self-reward: "I work hard; I deserve this." While treating yourself is a valid form of self-care, this mindset can spiral into overindulgence, creating a disconnect between short-term gratification and long-term goals. True self-care requires a balance—finding ways to indulge that support your emotional well-being without compromising your financial stability. Lasting joy often stems not from material possessions but from aligning spending with values that sustain your future.

- **Example 1: Retail Therapy's Temporary High**
  - After a stressful day, you decide to shop online for a "pick-me-up." You buy a designer handbag, and for a moment, you feel exhilarated. However, the euphoria fades quickly, replaced by guilt when the credit card bill arrives.

  - **Lesson:** Understand that the happiness from impulsive purchases is fleeting. Real, lasting joy often comes from experiences or savings that align with your goals.

- **Example 2: The Justification Spiral**
  - You convince yourself to buy an expensive gadget, saying, "I work hard; I deserve this." While self-care is important, this mindset can lead to overindulgence and financial instability if not balanced.

  - **Lesson:** Distinguish between genuine self-care and indulgence that undermines your long-term financial health. Treating yourself doesn't have to mean spending recklessly.

Part 3: Breaking Free From Social Pressures

In a world fueled by comparison, it's easy to fall into the trap of spending for the sake of appearances. At a friend's party, you might feel the sting of inadequacy when surrounded by designer-clad guests, prompting an impulsive splurge on an outfit for the next event—one that stretches your budget and leaves you questioning its worth. Similarly, scrolling through social media can amplify this pressure. Perfectly curated images of influencers basking on luxury vacations tempt you to book a trip you can't truly afford, all in an effort to "keep up." These moments serve as powerful reminders that confidence and fulfillment don't come from matching someone else's highlight reel. True self-worth is rooted in authenticity, not appearances. By redefining what it means to fit in and resisting the urge to compare, you can free yourself from the cycle of overspending and find joy in living authentically within your means.

- **Example 1:** Keeping Up Appearances
  - You attend a friend's party and feel self-conscious because others are dressed in designer clothes. To "fit in," you splurge on an outfit for the next event, even though it stretches your budget.

    - **Lesson:** Recognize that true confidence isn't tied to brands or appearances. Challenge yourself to redefine fitting in as being authentic rather than conforming to external expectations.

- **Example 2:** Social Media's Highlight Reel
  - Scrolling through Instagram, you see influencers flaunting luxury vacations, leading you to book an expensive trip to "keep up." Later, you feel financial strain and realize the trip wasn't necessary.

    - **Lesson:** Understand that social media often shows curated, unrealistic snapshots of life. Focus on your own journey and resist comparisons.

Part 4: The Neurological Pull of Consumerism

The allure of consumerism lies not just in the products we buy, but in the neurological reward system it taps into. When you stumble upon a "flash sale," the rush of dopamine makes the act of buying feel exhilarating—like you've just unlocked an exclusive treasure. Yet, once the buzz fades, you often realize the purchase wasn't needed, leaving regret in its wake. Similarly, online shopping platforms are masters of manipulation, keeping dopamine flowing with suggestions like "You might also like," nudging you to add more items to your cart. These tactics turn shopping into a game where the reward isn't the item itself but the fleeting thrill of acquisition. The lesson is clear: pause before impulse purchases, recognize these manipulative triggers, and stick to a plan. By reclaiming control, you shift from being a reactive consumer to an intentional spender.

- **Example 1:** Dopamine and Impulse Purchases
  - You walk into a store and see a "flash sale." The anticipation of getting a deal triggers dopamine, making the purchase feel rewarding. But later, you realize you didn't even need the item.

    - **Lesson:** Learn to pause before making purchases. Take time to assess whether the reward is worth the long-term impact on your finances.

- **Example 2:** The Shopping Cart Effect
    - Online retailers use tactics like "You might also like" or "Customers who bought this also purchased" to keep you adding to your cart. This strategy is designed to sustain dopamine spikes, leading to overspending.

    - **Lesson:** Be mindful of how shopping platforms manipulate your behavior. Stick to your list and avoid "browsing."

Part 5: Understanding Emotional Spending Triggers

Emotional spending often masquerades as self-care, but its aftermath can reveal misplaced priorities and lingering regret. Consider the celebration splurge: after receiving a well-deserved work bonus, you rush to reward yourself with a luxury watch. At first, it feels empowering—a tangible symbol of your success—but weeks later, as the thrill fades, you question whether that money could have bolstered your savings or investments instead. Then there's the stress purchase: a heated argument with a partner leads to an impulsive splurge on expensive home decor. For a fleeting moment, the new items fill the void, but they fail to address the unresolved tension. These scenarios teach us that emotional spending often offers only a temporary escape. By celebrating milestones with meaningful, long-term choices—such as investing in experiences or future goals—and addressing stress at its source, we can break the cycle of using spending as a quick fix and reclaim control over our financial and emotional well-being.

- **Example 1:** The Celebration Splurge
   - You receive a bonus at work and immediately spend it on a luxury watch, rationalizing it as a reward. Weeks later, you're left wondering if the money could have been better used for savings or investments.

   - **Lesson:** Celebrate milestones in meaningful ways that don't derail your financial goals. Experiences or contributions to long-term dreams can feel just as rewarding.

- **Example 2:** The Stress Purchase
   - After a fight with a partner, you buy expensive home decor to distract yourself. While it temporarily soothes the stress, the underlying issue remains unresolved.

   - **Lesson:** Address the root cause of emotional triggers instead of using purchases as a bandage.

Part 6: Building Emotional Awareness

Building emotional awareness around spending is a transformative step toward financial control. By journaling spending habits, you uncover patterns tied to emotions—stress prompting costly takeout or boredom fueling online shopping sprees. This newfound clarity empowers you to recognize triggers and interrupt harmful cycles before they spiral. Practicing delayed gratification further strengthens your resolve. When tempted to splurge on an expensive item, applying a simple 24-hour rule allows the initial urgency to fade. Often, you realize the desire was fleeting, and the decision to refrain feels empowering. Together, these practices cultivate mindfulness, turning impulsive spending into intentional choices that align with your goals.

- **Example 1:** Journaling Spending Habits
  - You start journaling your spending habits and notice patterns: stress leads to dining out, boredom to online shopping. This awareness helps you recognize and interrupt these cycles.

   - **Lesson:** Emotional awareness is the first step to breaking destructive spending habits. Track your behavior to identify triggers.

- **Example 2:** Practicing Delayed Gratification
  - When tempted to buy an expensive item, you implement a 24-hour rule. After waiting, the urgency fades, and you decide not to purchase.

   - **Lesson:** Delayed gratification helps curb impulsive spending and promotes thoughtful decision-making.

Summary of What Was Learned

The invisible hand of consumerism manipulates emotions, behaviors, and social pressures to encourage spending. By exploring these examples, readers learn:

1. Marketing strategies exploit psychological vulnerabilities, but awareness can neutralize their impact.

2. The "treat yourself" culture is seductive but often leads to regret unless balanced with purposeful spending.

3. Breaking free from social pressures requires redefining personal values and building financial confidence.

4. Consumerism taps into neurological responses, but mindfulness and patience can disrupt these patterns.

5. Emotional spending is often a reaction to deeper triggers; addressing the root cause can prevent unnecessary purchases.

6. Building emotional awareness and delaying gratification empower better financial decisions.

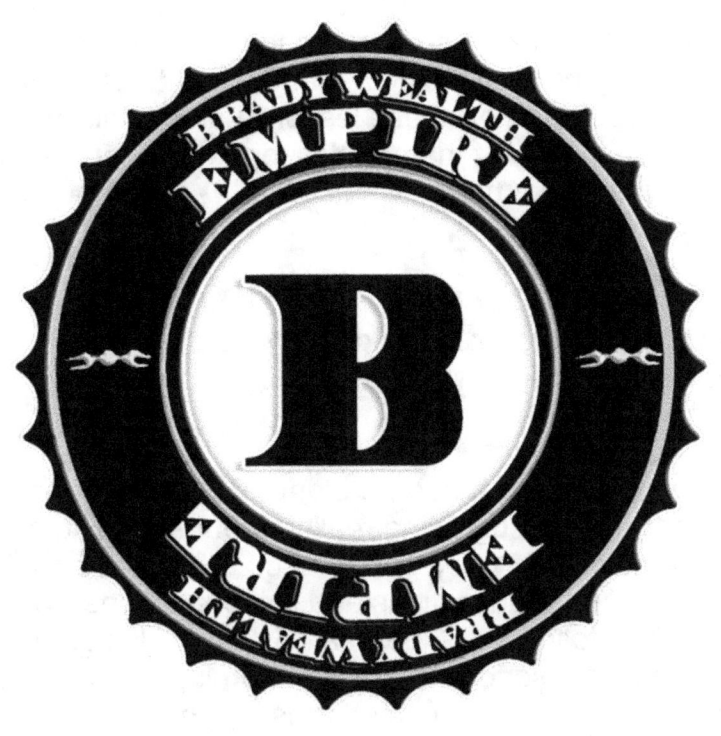

Chapter 3: "Facing the Truth: Your Spending Audit."

Chapter 3: Facing the Truth: Your Spending Audit

This chapter is divided into six parts, each focusing on a critical aspect of conducting a spending audit. Two relatable examples in each part will illustrate how these lessons can transform financial awareness. A summary at the end ties together what can be learned from these examples.

Part 1: The Importance of Tracking Every Dollar
Key Idea: Understanding where your money goes is the foundation of financial control.

Tracking every dollar is the cornerstone of financial empowerment, as it reveals the often-surprising reality of our spending habits. Take Lisa, for example—her daily coffee habit felt like a harmless treat until she tracked her transactions and discovered she was spending $150 a month, totaling $1,800 a year. Similarly, James unearthed a pile of forgotten subscriptions, from streaming platforms to a gym he hadn't visited in half a year, costing him $75 monthly. By canceling these, he reclaimed nearly $1,000 annually. These examples illustrate a vital lesson: small, seemingly insignificant expenses quietly snowball over time. When we track our money, we uncover these hidden drains and can redirect funds toward meaningful, intentional goals. It's a practice that not only fosters financial clarity but also builds the discipline needed to prioritize long-term satisfaction over fleeting indulgences.

Part 1: The Importance of Tracking Every Dollar
Key Idea: Understanding where your money goes is the foundation of financial control.

Example 1: The Coffee Conundrum
Lisa loves her daily coffee shop visits. She estimates she spends about $20 a week, but after tracking her transactions, she discovers she's actually spending $150 a month. The revelation shocks her—her "small indulgence" is costing her $1,800 a year.

Example 2: The Subscription Surprise
James decides to list all his recurring payments. He finds forgotten subscriptions—streaming platforms, a gym he hasn't visited in six months, and a forgotten magazine subscription—that total $75 a month. Canceling them instantly frees up nearly $1,000 annually.

What We Learn: Small, seemingly insignificant expenses add up over time. Tracking reveals these hidden costs, providing clarity and an opportunity to redirect money toward meaningful goals.

Part 2: Identifying Wasteful Patterns
Key Idea: Patterns of wasteful spending often go unnoticed until they are scrutinized.

Wasteful spending often hides in plain sight, buried beneath good intentions or small indulgences that feel harmless in the moment. Monica's weekly grocery trips, filled with ambitious plans for healthy meals, often end with spoiled produce and $200 a month wasted. By switching to a meal plan, she not only cuts costs but also eliminates the guilt of throwing food away. Marcus, on the other hand, is lured by the siren call of sales, convincing himself that discounted items are saving him money. Yet, his impulsive buys, totaling $300 a month, mostly collect dust. When he begins asking if he'd pay full price for each item, he breaks the cycle. These examples reveal how unchecked habits, driven by emotion or convenience, quietly drain finances. Identifying these patterns provides a powerful opportunity for change—an invitation to redirect money from fleeting whims to purposeful goals, where every dollar serves a meaningful purpose.

Example 1: The Grocery Guilt
Monica often throws out spoiled produce because she overbuys during her weekly grocery trips. After auditing her food expenses, she realizes she's wasting $200 a month on unused food. Switching to a meal plan saves her time and money.

Example 2: The Impulse Shopper

Marcus has a habit of buying things on sale, thinking he's saving money. When he reviews his spending, he sees that his "deals" add up to $300 a month on items he doesn't use. Marcus starts asking himself if he'd buy the item at full price, curbing his impulse buys.

What We Learn: Patterns like overbuying or impulsive shopping can be emotionally driven and go unnoticed. Identifying these behaviors allows for mindful corrections that prevent unnecessary spending.

Part 3: The Power of Awareness in Changing Habits
Key Idea: Awareness is transformative. Once you know where your money is going, you can make conscious decisions.

Awareness is the first step toward transformation. When Sophia discovered she was spending twice as much dining out as she thought, it wasn't just a shock—it was a wake-up call. By seeing the real numbers, she could consciously shift her habits, opting to cook at home and saving $200 a month while embracing a healthier lifestyle. Similarly, Jake's realization of his soaring fuel costs led him to rethink his transportation choices, swapping solo SUV drives for carpooling and public transit, slashing his expenses by $150 monthly. These examples show that awareness is not just about numbers; it's about accountability. Understanding where money is going empowers you to align spending with your true priorities and values. Patterns like impulsive shopping or small daily indulgences often go unnoticed, but tracking these expenses reveals opportunities for change. Delayed gratification becomes easier when clarity replaces denial, enabling mindful decisions that turn waste into wealth and goals into reality.

Example 1: Dining Out Dilemma
Sophia spends $500 a month dining out but believes it's closer to $250. Realizing the true cost, she commits to cooking at home three nights a week, saving $200 monthly while enjoying healthier meals.

Example 2: The Transportation Trap
Jake drives a gas-guzzling SUV, spending $400 a month on fuel. After seeing the numbers, he switches to carpooling and public

transport a few days a week, cutting his transportation costs by $150 monthly.

What We Learn: Awareness creates accountability. Seeing the actual numbers enables practical changes that align spending with priorities and values.

4: Practical Tools for Tracking and Auditing
Key Idea: Leverage tools to make tracking easier and more efficient.

Tracking and auditing your spending is a transformative practice, especially when leveraging practical tools like budgeting apps or cash systems. Emily's experience with a budgeting app like Mint reveals a surprising truth: 20% of her income vanishes into discretionary shopping. The app's automatic categorization and clear reports become her financial compass, helping her identify overspending patterns and set limits that align with her goals. Meanwhile, Tom's adoption of the cash envelope system turns budgeting into a tactile experience. By physically handling his money for categories like entertainment and groceries, he becomes more mindful of his choices, ensuring every dollar is spent with intention. Both approaches underscore a vital lesson: awareness breeds accountability. Tools simplify the process, revealing spending patterns and emotional triggers that often go unnoticed. They transform delayed gratification from a challenge into a strategy, empowering users to redirect funds toward meaningful goals and create financial habits rooted in clarity and purpose.

Example 1: Budgeting Apps
Emily downloads a budgeting app like Mint, which automatically categorizes her expenses. She's amazed to find that 20% of her income goes to discretionary shopping. The app's reports help her set limits and reduce unnecessary spending.

Example 2: The Cash Envelope System
Tom uses the envelope system for discretionary categories like entertainment and groceries. Physically seeing the money he has left makes him more deliberate about his choices, helping him stay within budget.

What We Learn: Tools simplify the process of tracking and provide visual clarity on spending habits. These systems can turn auditing into a seamless part of daily life.

Part 5: Overcoming Emotional Resistance
Key Idea: Facing spending habits can trigger guilt or fear, but overcoming these emotions is crucial for progress.

Overcoming emotional resistance is one of the most challenging yet transformative steps in taking control of your finances. Rachel's avoidance of her credit card statements, fueled by guilt and overwhelm, kept her trapped in a cycle of unnecessary interest payments. However, by confronting her fear and auditing her spending, she uncovered $200 a month in avoidable costs and took the first steps toward financial freedom with a repayment plan. Similarly, Kyle's reliance on retail therapy as a stress outlet masked deeper emotional triggers, leading to $500 in monthly spending on items that brought fleeting satisfaction. Recognizing these patterns allowed him to replace impulsive shopping with healthier coping mechanisms, ultimately saving money and fostering emotional growth. These examples show that while facing spending habits can stir guilt and fear, acknowledging them empowers change. By confronting emotional barriers, we can dismantle shame, embrace self-awareness, and take actionable steps toward lasting financial progress.

Example 1: The Credit Card Denial
Rachel avoids looking at her credit card statements because she feels overwhelmed by debt. Once she audits her spending, she realizes she's paying $200 a month in unnecessary interest. By creating a repayment plan, she starts regaining control.

Example 2: Retail Therapy Realization
Kyle uses shopping as a way to cope with stress. When he audits his finances, he sees that he's spent $500 a month on clothing he rarely wears. Recognizing the emotional trigger helps him find healthier coping mechanisms, saving money in the process.

What We Learn: Emotional resistance is common but acknowledging it is empowering. Auditing spending helps dismantle fear and shame, turning awareness into actionable change.

Part 6: Turning Insights Into Action
Key Idea: The ultimate goal of auditing is to create a proactive financial plan.

Auditing your finances is more than just identifying leaks in your budget—it's a transformative tool that empowers you to take purposeful action. Melissa's story illustrates the peace of mind that comes from redirecting saved expenses into an emergency fund, turning what was once wasted money into a $900 safety net in just six months. Ethan, on the other hand, used his newfound awareness to realign his spending with his dreams, cutting $200 from entertainment to create a travel fund, ultimately booking the trip he'd always envisioned. These examples show that auditing is the gateway to financial empowerment; the clarity it provides allows you to prioritize what truly matters and actively shape a future that reflects your goals and values.

Example 1: Redirecting Savings
After auditing her spending, Melissa reallocates the $150 she saved from canceling unused subscriptions toward an emergency fund. Within six months, she's built a $900 cushion that provides peace of mind.

Example 2: Budgeting for Priorities
After tracking his spending, Ethan realizes he's not saving for his goal of traveling. By cutting $200 from entertainment and dining out, he creates a dedicated travel fund and books his dream trip within a year.

What We Learn: Auditing is a means to an end—awareness enables action. The real value lies in using insights to align spending with your long-term goals and values.

Summary of What Was Learned

1. Tracking Creates Clarity: Understanding where every dollar goes uncovers surprising patterns and opportunities to save.

2. Small Changes Add Up: Addressing hidden costs and wasteful habits leads to significant financial improvement over time.

3. Awareness Drives Change: Once aware of spending habits, people can make intentional decisions that align with their priorities.

4. Emotions Matter: Spending is often tied to feelings. Identifying and addressing emotional triggers is key to sustainable habits.

5. Action is Empowering: Auditing is just the beginning—redirecting money toward meaningful goals transforms financial health and emotional well-being.

Chapter 4: "The Power of No: Reclaiming Control Over Your Wallet."

Chapter 4: The Power of No: Reclaiming Control Over Your Wallet

Part 1: Setting Boundaries in a World That Demands More

1 Example 1: Declining a Social Invitation

A friend invites you to an extravagant dinner at a high-end restaurant. You feel pressured to attend because everyone else in your circle is going, but the price tag doesn't align with your budget. You respectfully decline, suggesting a more budget-friendly coffee meetup instead.

What was learned? Saying "no" doesn't mean isolating yourself; it means prioritizing your financial health. Setting boundaries fosters creative alternatives that maintain relationships while protecting your goals.

2. Example 2: Skipping the Seasonal Sale

A flashy email announces a "once-in-a-lifetime" sale. You're tempted to buy clothes you don't truly need, driven by the fear of missing out. Instead, you delete the email and remind yourself that owning fewer but purposeful items brings more satisfaction.

What was learned? Marketing thrives on urgency and scarcity, but saying "no" allows you to reclaim control over your decisions rather than being manipulated by external triggers.

Summary:

Setting boundaries involves recognizing the pressures that compel you to overspend and asserting control over these situations. It's about reclaiming your time, money, and energy from external demands.

Part 2: The Freedom of Saying No to Things That Don't Matter

1. Example 1: Canceling Unused Subscriptions

You realize you're paying for three streaming services but primarily use only one. After evaluating your usage, you cancel the unnecessary subscriptions, saving $20 a month.

What was learned? Small recurring expenses add up over time. Saying "no" to services you no longer use liberates your finances for things that truly matter.

2. Example 2: Choosing Experiences Over Material Goods

Instead of buying another designer handbag you don't need, you decide to spend that money on a weekend getaway with your family. The memories created far outweigh the fleeting joy of the purchase.

What was learned? Prioritizing experiences over possessions creates lasting joy and aligns your spending with what genuinely enriches your life.

Summary:

Saying "no" to things that don't align with your values frees you to spend on what truly matters, fostering long-term satisfaction over short-term gratification.

Part 3: Redefining What Brings You Joy

1. Example 1: Simplifying Holiday Spending

During the holidays, you decide to scale back on extravagant gifts, opting instead to write heartfelt letters or give meaningful but modest items. Your family responds with appreciation for the thought behind the gifts.

What was learned? True joy isn't tied to the monetary value of what you give; it's found in the intention and connection that accompanies the act.

2. Example 2: Decluttering Your Space
You take a weekend to declutter your closet, donating clothes you haven't worn in years. As you pare down, you feel lighter and rediscover joy in the simplicity of a more organized space.

What was learned? Owning less often brings clarity and joy. Letting go of unnecessary possessions allows you to appreciate what you have and focus on what truly adds value.

Summary:

Redefining joy involves separating real happiness from consumer-driven notions of success. Simplicity and meaningful connections often lead to greater fulfillment.

Part 4: Overcoming Fear of Missing Out (FOMO)

1. Example 1: Skipping a Tech Upgrade

A new smartphone launches with much fanfare, and your friends rush to upgrade. You evaluate your current phone, realize it works perfectly fine, and decide to skip the hype.

What was learned? The fear of missing out can lead to unnecessary spending. Pausing to assess real need versus perceived social pressure builds confidence in your decisions.

2. Example 2: Ignoring Flashy Ads for Limited Editions

A luxury brand drops a limited-edition item that everyone seems to want. You're tempted but remind yourself that exclusivity is a marketing ploy. You stick to your savings plan instead.

What was learned? Resisting FOMO helps you focus on long-term goals instead of being swayed by fleeting trends and marketing tactics.

Summary:

Overcoming FOMO is about recognizing how external pressures manipulate your emotions and standing firm in your commitment to what truly matters.

Part 5: Building Confidence Through Financial Wins

1. Example 1: Saying No to a Major Purchase

You've been considering a new car because yours is older but still reliable. After weighing the costs, you decide to keep your current car and allocate the money you would've spent on a down payment toward your emergency fund.

What was learned? Confidence grows when you make financially responsible decisions that align with your priorities. Every win reinforces your ability to manage money effectively.

2. Example 2: Creating a Fun Budget

You decide to cap your entertainment spending at $50 a month. By doing so, you find creative ways to enjoy yourself—like hosting potluck dinners or exploring free local events—without feeling deprived.

What was learned? Financial wins aren't about deprivation; they're about creativity and intention. Setting limits fosters empowerment and control.

Summary:

Building confidence comes from small financial victories that validate your choices. Over time, these wins reinforce your ability to manage money wisely and reduce the emotional strain of spending.

Part 6: The Ripple Effect of Saying No

1. **Example 1: Inspiring Family to Budget**
2.

After implementing boundaries and cutting unnecessary spending, you share your successes with family. Inspired, they start reevaluating their finances and adopting similar habits.

What was learned? Your financial discipline can positively impact others, creating a ripple effect of smarter spending within your community.

2. Example 2: Investing in Long-Term Goals

By consistently saying "no" to frivolous expenses, you save enough to start contributing to a retirement account. The peace of mind this brings encourages you to stay committed to your financial plan.

What was learned? Saying "no" is a pathway to bigger opportunities. Each decision to save builds momentum toward long-term security and financial freedom.

Summary:

The power of "no" extends beyond your wallet. It influences others and sets the stage for a future filled with possibilities.

Final Summary of Chapter 4

Saying "no" is a radical act of self-care in a world that constantly demands more. Through small but deliberate choices, you reclaim control over your wallet, align your spending with your values, and experience the freedom and joy of purposeful living. Each "no" builds the foundation for a future of empowerment, security, and fulfillment.

Chapter 5: "Mastering Minimalism: Spending With Purpose."

Chapter 5: Mastering Minimalism: Spending With Purpose

Part 1: The Art of Deliberate Spending

Example 1: The Coffee Habit

Jane used to buy a $5 coffee every morning without thinking. Over a year, this added up to $1,825. After tracking her expenses, Jane decided to make her coffee at home. She invested $50 in a quality French press and now spends $0.50 per cup. This small change saved her over $1,500 annually and gave her more control over her mornings.

Example 2: The Impulse Shopper

Mike often bought items during online flash sales, believing he was saving money. When his closet overflowed with unworn clothes, he realized these "savings" cost him over $2,000 a year. By implementing a 24-hour rule before purchasing, he dramatically reduced his spending, saving both money and mental clutter.

Lesson Learned:

Deliberate spending begins with awareness. By pausing to consider purchases, you prevent unnecessary spending and align your money with your priorities. It's not about depriving yourself but about making intentional choices that serve your long-term goals.

Part 2: How Owning Less Can Feel Like Having More

Example 1: Sarah's Decluttered Kitchen

Sarah had drawers stuffed with gadgets she never used—avocado slicers, yogurt makers, and old utensils. She donated everything except for her essentials, like a chef's knife and skillet. The streamlined space made cooking enjoyable and saved her from buying duplicates.

Example 2: The Capsule Wardrobe

Lauren was overwhelmed by her closet filled with clothes she didn't wear. She created a capsule wardrobe of 30 versatile, high-quality items. Not only did this save her time and reduce stress, but she also discovered she spent less on fast fashion because she appreciated what she already had.

Lesson Learned:

Owning less can reduce stress, save time, and improve your quality of life. Minimalism isn't about scarcity; it's about creating space for what truly matters and letting go of excess that distracts you from joy.

Part 3: Choosing Quality Over Quantity

Example 1: The Winter Coat Investment

Josh used to buy a new $100 winter coat every year because they wore out quickly. After doing some research, he spent $400 on a high-quality coat with a lifetime warranty. Five years later, the coat is still in excellent condition, and he hasn't needed to buy another. Over time, he saved $100 per year.

Example 2: Kitchen Appliances That Last

Emily replaced her $30 blender three times in two years. Frustrated, she purchased a $200 high-performance blender. Not only did it last longer, but it worked better, reducing her frustration and saving her money in the long term.

Lesson Learned:

Investing in quality items often saves money over time and enhances daily experiences. High-quality products reduce the need for replacements, making them both cost-effective and satisfying to use.

Part 4: Prioritizing Experiences Over Things

Example 1: The Travel Enthusiast

Instead of buying designer bags, Kendra saved $1,500 for a two-week trip to Europe. The memories, friendships, and cultural experiences she gained were priceless compared to the fleeting joy of material possessions.

Example 2: Family Game Night

Mark used to spend hundreds on new electronics for his kids. He switched gears and spent $50 on board games for family nights. His children cherished the bonding time, and the entire family felt closer and more fulfilled.

Lesson Learned:

Experiences often provide deeper and longer-lasting satisfaction than material goods. They create memories, strengthen relationships, and contribute to personal growth in ways that possessions cannot.

Part 5: Simplifying Your Financial Habits

Example 1: Automating Savings

Lisa struggled to save consistently. By setting up automatic transfers to a savings account on payday, she no longer had to think about it. Over six months, she accumulated $3,000 without stress or effort.

Example 2: Subscription Clean-Up

Dan canceled streaming services he rarely used, saving $60 monthly. Instead of feeling deprived, he used free alternatives like public libraries and ad-supported platforms, which met his entertainment needs without the extra cost.

Lesson Learned:

Simplifying financial habits, like automating savings or reducing recurring expenses, reduces decision fatigue and creates a sense of control over your finances. It's about making money management effortless.

Part 6: Aligning Purchases With Values

Example 1: Supporting Local Businesses

Mia decided to shift her grocery budget to local farmers' markets. Although slightly more expensive, she felt pride knowing her money supported small farms. She ate fresher, healthier food and enjoyed the connection to her community.

Example 2: The Ethical Shopper

James avoided fast fashion after learning about its environmental impact. He chose to buy from sustainable brands. Though pricier upfront, these clothes lasted longer and aligned with his values, making him feel empowered.

Lesson Learned:

Aligning spending with values creates a sense of purpose and fulfillment. It shifts consumption from a mindless activity to a meaningful expression of your principles, enhancing satisfaction with each purchase.

Summary of Lessons From the Examples

1. Awareness Leads to Control: Pausing to reflect on purchases transforms spending into a purposeful act.

2. Minimalism Reduces Stress: Owning less creates space for joy, clarity, and financial savings.

3. Quality Over Quantity Saves Money: Investing in durable, well-made items reduces long-term costs and enhances daily life.

4. Experiences Outweigh Things: Memorable experiences bring lasting happiness, unlike fleeting satisfaction from material goods.

5. Simplicity is Empowering: Automating finances and reducing recurring expenses creates a sense of control.

6. Values-Driven Spending Feels Good: Spending in alignment with your principles brings fulfillment and pride.

Chapter 6: "Smart Cuts: Where to Trim Without Pain."

Chapter 6: Smart Cuts: Where to Trim Without Pain

Part 1: Hidden Savings in Everyday Expenses
Everyday expenses are often the most overlooked opportunities for savings, but identifying these small leaks can lead to significant gains.

1. Example 1: Subscription Overload
   Sarah realized she was paying for five streaming services but only regularly used two. By canceling the unused ones, she saved $30 monthly, or $360 annually.

   Lesson Learned: Regularly auditing subscriptions can uncover hidden expenses, allowing you to reallocate those funds toward savings or more meaningful investments.

2. Example 2: The Morning Coffee Ritual
   David bought a $5 latte every workday, totaling $100 monthly. After switching to brewing coffee at home, he reduced this expense to $10 monthly, saving $1,080 annually.

   Lesson Learned: Small, habitual expenses like coffee runs add up over time. Simple substitutions can lead to substantial savings without feeling deprived.

Summary: Everyday expenses often go unnoticed, but taking time to evaluate and reduce unnecessary costs can create immediate and impactful savings.

Part 2: The Big Three: Housing
Housing is often the largest expense in a budget, and even small adjustments can yield significant savings.

1. Example 1: Negotiating Rent
   Carla negotiated her lease renewal and secured a $100 monthly reduction. This amounted to $1,200 in yearly savings without moving or sacrificing her quality of living.

   Lesson Learned: Many landlords are open to negotiation, especially if you're a reliable tenant. Asking for a reduction or perks like free parking can save substantial money.

2. Example 2: Downsizing Without Downgrading

Mike moved from a two-bedroom apartment to a one-bedroom unit within the same building. He saved $400 monthly and used the extra space for decluttering his life.

Lesson Learned: Downsizing doesn't mean giving up comfort—it can be an opportunity to rethink your space and financial priorities.

Summary: Housing adjustments don't have to be drastic to make a difference. From negotiating rent to reconsidering your space needs, housing expenses offer room for optimization.

Part 3: The Big Three: Transportation

Transportation costs, including car payments, fuel, and maintenance, can consume a large part of your budget. Smart changes can lead to long-term savings.

1. Example 1: Carpooling Saves Cash
Jenny started carpooling with coworkers three days a week, cutting her fuel expenses by 40%. Over the year, she saved $720.

Lesson Learned: Sharing transportation can significantly reduce costs while fostering connections and environmental benefits.

2. Example 2: Switching to Public Transit
Tom replaced his car commute with public transit, saving on fuel, parking, and insurance costs. His total savings exceeded $2,500 annually.

Lesson Learned: Exploring alternatives like public transportation can lead to both financial and lifestyle benefits, such as reduced stress and downtime for personal activities.

Summary: Transportation is a prime area for savings. Sharing rides or switching to public transit can free up funds while enhancing your quality of life.

Part 4: The Big Three: Food
Food expenses are a daily necessity, but they're also ripe with opportunities for smart cuts without sacrificing quality.

1. **Example 1:** Meal Prepping for Success
   Karen started meal prepping on Sundays, reducing her weekly grocery and dining expenses by $50. Over a year, she saved $2,600 while eating healthier meals.

   Lesson Learned: Planning meals not only saves money but also helps control portion sizes and improve overall health.

2. **Example 2:** Dining Out Strategically
   Rather than frequenting expensive restaurants weekly, Adam limited himself to dining out once a month, saving $200 monthly.

   Lesson Learned: Reducing dining out doesn't mean eliminating enjoyment—it's about creating balance and being selective about when and where to splurge.

Summary: Food expenses can be controlled through planning and moderation, turning a high-cost necessity into a manageable part of your budget.

Part 5: Simple Lifestyle Tweaks That Add Up
Small, everyday changes often yield some of the most surprising savings.

1. **Example 1:** Switching Utility Providers
   Lisa switched her energy provider to one offering lower rates, saving $25 monthly. Over a year, that added up to $300.

   Lesson Learned: Utility costs are often negotiable or have cheaper alternatives. A little research can lead to significant savings.

2. **Example 2:** Embracing Secondhand Shopping
   John replaced his habit of buying new clothing with secondhand shopping, saving $600 annually while still maintaining a stylish wardrobe.

   Lesson Learned: Pre-owned items often deliver the same utility and satisfaction at a fraction of the cost.

Summary: Small, seemingly minor adjustments in everyday life, from utilities to shopping habits, can compound into meaningful financial relief.
Part 6: Automation for Effortless Savings

Automating your savings efforts ensures consistency and eliminates the risk of accidental overspending.

1. **Example 1:** Auto-Saving 10% of Income

Emily set up an automatic transfer to her savings account each payday, ensuring she consistently saved $200 monthly. Over a year, she accumulated $2,400 effortlessly.

Lesson Learned: Automation takes the emotion out of saving and helps establish consistent habits without requiring daily discipline.

2. Example 2: Bill Payment Automation

Greg automated his bill payments, avoiding late fees and missed payments, saving $120 annually.

Lesson Learned: Automating recurring expenses reduces stress, eliminates penalties, and ensures peace of mind.

Summary: Automation turns good intentions into reliable outcomes, allowing you to focus on other areas of financial improvement.

Comprehensive Summary of Chapter 6

- **Key Takeaway:** Saving doesn't have to feel restrictive. By making small, targeted adjustments in everyday expenses, the "Big Three," and adopting simple tweaks, you can significantly reduce costs while maintaining your quality of life.

- **Emotional Impact:** These strategies empower readers to take control of their finances with confidence, transforming small sacrifices into opportunities for long-term financial stability.

Chapter 7: "Smart Cuts: Where to Trim Without Pain."

Chapter 7: Beating Subscription Fatigue

Part 1: Identifying and Canceling Unnecessary Services

1. Example 1: The Forgotten Streaming Service
   - A reader realizes they are subscribed to five streaming platforms but consistently use only two. After auditing their usage, they cancel three, saving $45 monthly.
   - Lesson Learned: Regularly reviewing subscription usage helps eliminate waste. What seems like a small monthly expense quickly adds up when multiple unused services accumulate.

2. Example 2: The Gym Membership That Doesn't Fit
   - A gym membership costing $40/month goes unused because the reader prefers at-home workouts. They cancel and replace it with free YouTube workout videos.
   - Lesson Learned: It's important to align spending with actual habits and needs. Canceling a service you're not using doesn't mean giving up your goals; it means finding a better fit.

Summary: Identifying and canceling unnecessary services teaches that small, unnoticed expenses can quietly drain finances. Reviewing spending habits and aligning them with actual use ensures money is spent intentionally.

Part 2: Using Free or Low-Cost Alternatives

1. Example 1: Free Digital Libraries
   - A reader paying $15/month for an audiobook service discovers their local library offers free access to thousands of audiobooks through an app like Libby. They switch, saving $180 annually.
   - Lesson Learned: There are often free or community-supported alternatives to paid services. Exploring these options can provide the same benefits without the cost.

2. Example 2: Free Software for Productivity

- Instead of renewing a $10/month subscription for a task management app, the reader switches to a free alternative like Trello or Notion, saving $120 annually.
- Lesson Learned: Many free apps offer similar functionality to paid services. A little research can uncover tools that meet your needs without sacrificing quality.

Summary: Free and low-cost alternatives can often replace paid services without compromising value. By exploring these options, readers can maintain or enhance their lifestyle while reducing expenses.

Part 3: Automating to Avoid Accidental Renewals

1. Example 1: Credit Card Alerts
- A reader sets up notifications on their credit card for recurring payments. This alert helps them identify an unused $7.99 subscription they forgot to cancel, saving $96 annually.
- Lesson Learned: Automating alerts creates a safety net for catching forgotten subscriptions. Awareness is the first step toward regaining control.

2. Example 2: Prepaid Gift Cards for Trials
- Instead of using a credit card for a free trial, a reader uses a prepaid gift card with a low balance. When the trial ends, the auto-renew fails, avoiding unexpected charges.
- Lesson Learned: Using smart automation strategies or limited payment methods can prevent unwanted charges and reinforce intentional spending habits.

Summary: Automation is a powerful tool to protect against accidental renewals. By setting up systems to monitor or limit subscriptions, readers can prevent unnecessary expenses effortlessly.

Part 4: Simplifying the Subscription Landscape

1. **Example 1: Bundling Services**
   - A reader consolidates their streaming services by subscribing to a bundle package that includes their favorite platforms, saving $20 monthly.
   - Lesson Learned: Bundling related services reduces costs and simplifies management, ensuring you're not paying for overlapping features.

2. **Example 2: Family or Group Sharing**
   - A group of friends shares a premium family plan for a music streaming service, splitting the $15 cost and reducing individual expenses to $3 monthly.
   - Lesson Learned: Sharing services is a collaborative way to cut costs without losing access to the features you value.

Summary: Simplifying subscriptions through bundling or sharing reduces costs and complexity. These strategies align with a minimalist financial mindset, focusing on efficiency.

Part 5: Mindset Shift: Wants vs. Needs

1. **Example 1:** Reevaluating Entertainment Priorities
   - A reader cancels all paid entertainment subscriptions and decides to spend more time enjoying outdoor activities, reading, or socializing. They save $50 monthly and feel more fulfilled.

   - **Lesson Learned:** Differentiating between wants and needs helps prioritize spending on what truly enriches your life.

2. **Example 2:** Monthly Reflection Practice
   - A reader begins a monthly reflection practice to evaluate their subscriptions. They ask, Does this add value to my life? This leads to canceling a barely used gaming subscription, saving $10 monthly.

   - **Lesson Learned:** Regular self-assessment ensures spending aligns with current priorities and prevents unnecessary financial drains.

Summary: Shifting your mindset to assess needs versus wants fosters intentional spending. By questioning the true value of subscriptions, readers can focus on what enhances their lives.

Part 6: Tracking Progress and Celebrating Wins

1. Example 1: Tracking Subscription Savings
   - A reader tracks their canceled subscriptions over a year and realizes they've saved over $600, which they use to pay down debt.

   - **Lesson Learned:** Tracking progress makes savings tangible and motivates further financial improvements.

2. Example 2: Rewarding Financial Discipline
   - After saving money through smarter subscription management, a reader treats themselves to a guilt-free experience, like a weekend getaway.

   - **Lesson Learned:** Celebrating small financial wins reinforces positive behavior and creates a sustainable cycle of progress.

Summary: Tracking savings and celebrating successes reinforces the value of intentional financial decisions. These practices build motivation and satisfaction, encouraging long-term habits.

Overall Summary of Chapter 7

By identifying unnecessary services, exploring free alternatives, automating renewals, simplifying choices, shifting mindsets, and tracking progress, readers develop a holistic approach to conquering subscription fatigue. This chapter transforms a passive expense into an active opportunity to save and redirect money toward meaningful goals.

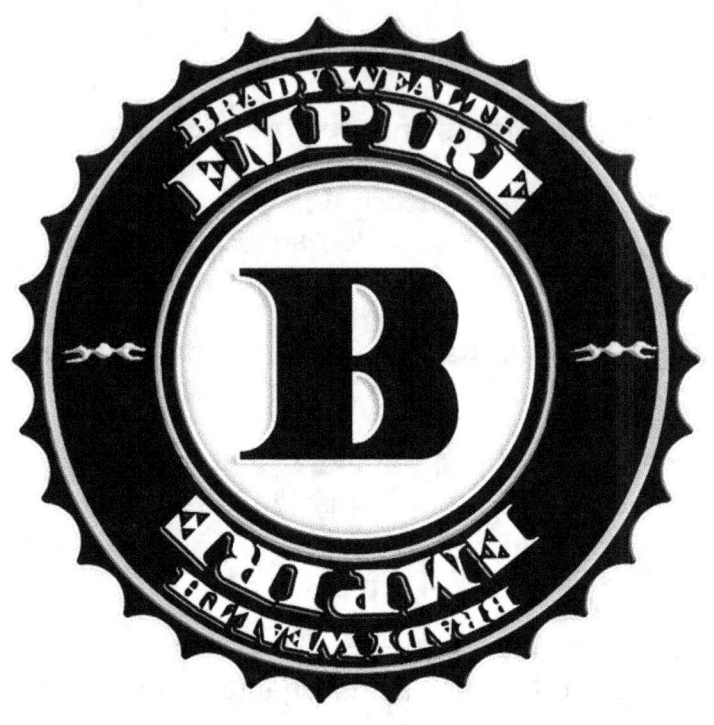

Chapter 8: "Building a Fortress of Savings."

Chapter 8: Building a Fortress of Savings

Part 1: The Emotional Security of an Emergency Fund

An emergency fund is more than a bank account; it's a shield against life's unpredictability. Imagine the peace of mind that comes from knowing you can handle unexpected expenses without spiraling into debt. Whether it's a sudden medical bill or an urgent home repair, this fund becomes your financial safety net. It's the calm reassurance that, no matter what life throws your way, you have a plan in place. The emotional weight of financial uncertainty is lifted, allowing you to focus on living rather than worrying.

Beyond practicality, an emergency fund builds confidence. It's a statement of self-reliance and preparedness, a tangible representation of your ability to take control of your future. When you create this cushion, you're no longer at the mercy of emergencies, which often feel like financial earthquakes. Instead, you become the calm amid the chaos, knowing you've prepared for the inevitable storms.

Example 1: Sarah, a single mother, faced a $1,200 car repair bill after her car broke down unexpectedly. Thanks to her emergency fund, she paid for the repair without resorting to a high-interest credit card.

Example 2: James, a freelancer, saved three months' worth of expenses in his emergency fund. When a major client suddenly canceled their contract, James had the resources to cover his bills while finding new work.

Summary of Examples: These stories highlight how an emergency fund turns crises into manageable inconveniences, eliminating panic and fostering financial resilience.

Part 2: How Small Savings Lead to Big Wins

Small savings often feel insignificant, but over time, they create a profound impact. The beauty of incremental saving is its accessibility—anyone can start with what they have. It's the daily habit of putting away even a few dollars that compounds into substantial financial security. These small wins create momentum, reinforcing your confidence in your ability to save and showing how little changes lead to big results.

The act of saving small amounts also shifts your mindset. Instead of focusing on what you lack, you begin to celebrate what you've achieved. Each dollar saved is a step closer to your financial goals, proof that progress is within reach. By breaking the overwhelming goal of savings into bite-sized chunks, you make financial security achievable and rewarding.

Example 1: Rachel set up an automatic transfer of $5 a day into her savings account. In a year, she amassed $1,825, enough to cover a family emergency without stress.

Example 2: Marcus saved the change from every purchase using a round-up savings app. Over two years, he accumulated $950, which he used to pay for a sudden dental procedure.

Summary of Examples: These examples illustrate how small, consistent efforts create significant financial rewards over time, turning savings into a manageable and achievable habit.

Part 3: Creating a Buffer for Life's Unexpected Moments

Life's unpredictability isn't a question of if, but when. An emergency fund acts as a buffer, softening the blow of unforeseen events. Without this financial cushion, unexpected expenses can derail your budget, forcing you into debt or difficult choices. Having a buffer in place ensures that you can respond to these situations with confidence and clarity rather than panic.

Building this buffer doesn't mean expecting the worst; it means preparing for it. It's the difference between reacting to a crisis and navigating it with control. Whether it's an unexpected job loss, a medical emergency, or a major home repair, a buffer fund provides the flexibility to adapt, protect your assets, and maintain your financial goals.

Example 1: After losing her job, Anita used her emergency fund to cover rent and utilities for three months, giving her the breathing room to find a better opportunity without rushing into a low-paying job.

Example 2: John and Lisa faced a $3,000 roof repair after a storm. Thanks to their buffer fund, they handled the expense without dipping into their retirement savings or taking on debt.

Summary of Examples: These cases show how a buffer fund transforms unexpected challenges into manageable situations, preserving financial stability and reducing stress during tough times.

Part 4: The Psychological Impact of Savings

Savings aren't just financial; they're emotional. The act of saving creates a sense of accomplishment and control, reducing anxiety about money. Knowing you have a safety net gives you a sense of independence, empowering you to make decisions without fear of financial repercussions. This psychological shift is as valuable as the money itself.

Moreover, saving teaches discipline and delayed gratification. Each time you prioritize savings over a fleeting purchase, you're reinforcing your ability to focus on long-term goals. This creates a positive feedback loop where saving feels rewarding and natural, building a foundation for a secure and confident financial future.

Example 1: David, once overwhelmed by financial stress, began saving small amounts each week. Over time, he noticed a shift in his confidence and a significant reduction in his anxiety about money.

Example 2: Maria, who struggled with impulse spending, began tracking her savings progress. Seeing her account grow gave her a sense of pride and control she'd never experienced before.

Summary of Examples: These stories highlight the profound emotional benefits of savings, demonstrating how financial preparation enhances mental well-being.

Part 5: Building Savings Habits That Stick

Sustainable savings require consistent habits. The key is automating the process, removing the temptation to spend before you save. By treating savings as a non-negotiable expense—like rent or utilities—you make it an integral part of your financial routine. This consistency builds habits that last a lifetime, creating a financial cushion almost effortlessly.

Another crucial habit is setting realistic goals. Break your savings target into manageable steps, celebrating small milestones along the way. This approach keeps you motivated and ensures that savings don't feel like a burden but an achievement.

Example 1: Emily automated 10% of her paycheck into her savings account. Over two years, she saved $12,000 without ever feeling the pinch.

Example 2: Chris set a goal to save $1,000 in six months by cutting out takeout meals and redirecting that money to his savings. He reached his goal early and felt empowered to aim higher.

Summary of Examples: These examples underscore the importance of automation and goal-setting in creating lasting savings habits, proving that consistency is key to financial success.

Part 6: The Freedom Savings Brings

Savings are more than money; they're freedom. They free you from the fear of financial instability and open the door to opportunities you might otherwise hesitate to pursue. With savings, you can take risks—whether it's starting a business, traveling, or pursuing a passion—without the constant worry of how you'll pay the bills.

This freedom also extends to relationships and personal growth. Savings give you the independence to say no to toxic environments or situations that don't serve you. They provide the foundation to build a life of purpose and security, empowering you to chase your dreams without compromise.

Example 1: When Laura decided to switch careers, her savings gave her the confidence to take a six-month unpaid internship, which eventually led to her dream job.

Example 2: Tom used his emergency fund to move out of a stressful living situation, finding a safer and more supportive environment for his mental health.

Summary of Examples: These examples illustrate how savings empower people to take control of their lives, unlocking freedom, choice, and the ability to pursue meaningful opportunities.

Conclusion of Chapter 8

This chapter emphasizes the multifaceted benefits of building a fortress of savings—financial stability, emotional security, and the freedom to live on your terms. Through practical steps and real-life examples, it shows that saving isn't just about money; it's about creating a life of resilience, confidence, and possibility.

Chapter 9: " From Scarcity to Abundance: Changing Your Money Story."

Chapter 9: From Scarcity to Abundance: Changing Your Money Story

1. Shifting Your Mindset From Deprivation to Empowerment

The scarcity mindset thrives on fear—the fear of never having enough, of losing what you have, and of falling behind. It keeps you in a cycle of anxiety, where every dollar spent feels like a loss. This mindset often stems from past experiences of lack, whether financial instability in childhood or ongoing struggles as an adult. The key to breaking free is reframing how you see money—not as something that controls you, but as a tool you control. Empowerment comes when you focus on what your money can do for you, whether it's securing your future, achieving your goals, or granting you peace of mind.

Empowerment means celebrating every financial win, no matter how small. By focusing on what you can do rather than what you can't, you regain a sense of agency over your money. This shift doesn't mean ignoring financial challenges but tackling them with confidence, knowing each decision brings you closer to abundance. For example, choosing to save $20 a week might seem trivial, but over time, it builds momentum—and belief—in your ability to create change.

Examples:

1. Lisa's Savings Jar: Lisa always felt deprived when saving, but she reframed it as a game. Each week, she added $10 to a jar and celebrated by writing a sticky note of something she was grateful for. Over six months, she saved $260 and felt a deep sense of accomplishment.

2. John's Budget Wins: John feared budgeting because it felt restrictive. Instead, he renamed his budget his "Dream Fund" and allocated money for small pleasures like a coffee outing. He found joy in knowing he was planning for both the present and future.

Summary: Shifting from deprivation to empowerment transforms saving into a positive experience. Both Lisa and John discovered that celebrating small steps made the journey feel achievable and rewarding.

2. The Joy of Watching Your Savings Grow

There's something deeply satisfying about seeing your savings account balance rise. It's a tangible representation of your discipline, growth, and future security. Watching your money grow gives you a sense of control in a world where so much feels uncertain. Each deposit, no matter how small, is a step toward your goals—whether it's a dream vacation, an emergency fund, or financial independence.

The process of saving can transform from a chore into a source of pride. Think of your savings as planting seeds in a garden. At first, it seems like nothing is happening, but over time, the sprouts appear, and soon you have a flourishing landscape. This growth creates a feedback loop of positivity: the more you save, the more motivated you feel to continue. Each milestone brings a rush of joy, reinforcing your belief in the power of small, consistent actions.

Examples:
1. Sarah's Travel Dreams: Sarah started saving $50 a month for a trip to Europe. Over two years, she watched her account grow to $1,200. The joy of seeing the balance climb kept her motivated, and she felt immense pride when she finally booked her tickets.

2. Tony's Emergency Fund: Tony set a goal of saving $500 for emergencies. Each time he deposited money, he tracked his progress with a graph on his fridge. Watching the line climb higher gave him a sense of accomplishment and control over his financial future.

Summary: The act of saving is not just practical—it's deeply rewarding. Sarah and Tony found joy and motivation by celebrating their growing savings, transforming financial habits into positive reinforcement

3. How to Turn Financial Fear Into Confidence

Financial fear can feel paralyzing. It stems from uncertainty—unexpected expenses, mounting debt, or the fear of failure. This fear often leads to avoidance, which only exacerbates the problem. The antidote to fear is action, and the first step is facing your finances head-on. Knowledge is power, and understanding your financial situation—even if it's uncomfortable—lays the foundation for change.

Confidence grows as you take control of your money. Creating a budget, setting goals, or addressing debt might feel daunting, but each small success builds momentum. The act of confronting fear transforms it into courage. Confidence isn't about having all the answers—it's about trusting your ability to make smart financial decisions, even in the face of challenges.

Examples:
1. Emma's Debt Plan: Emma was terrified to look at her credit card balance. But after listing her debts and creating a repayment plan, she felt more in control. Paying off her first $500 gave her a surge of confidence to tackle the rest.

2. Marcus's Budget Confidence: Marcus avoided budgeting because he feared seeing how little he earned. Once he created a budget, he realized he could save $100 a month. This small victory gave him the confidence to set bigger goals.

Summary: Turning financial fear into confidence requires action and small wins. Emma and Marcus faced their fears and discovered that clarity and progress were far more empowering than avoidance.

4. Shifting From Consumer to Creator

Scarcity teaches you to see yourself as a consumer, always taking but never creating. Abundance flips the script, encouraging you to think of money as a way to build something lasting. When you approach finances from a creator's mindset, you see opportunities instead of limitations. This perspective empowers you to create wealth, whether through investments, skills, or new ventures.

Being a creator is about actively shaping your financial story. Instead of feeling powerless, you embrace the role of architect in your financial future. This shift transforms money from something that controls you into a tool you wield with purpose. You begin to see that every dollar is an opportunity to invest in yourself, your dreams, and your future.

Examples:

1. Maya's Side Hustle: Maya started selling handmade candles as a creative outlet. Within a year, she turned it into a small business, earning $500 a month. This shift from consumer to creator made her see money as a tool for building her dreams.

2. David's Investment Journey: David used to spend his bonuses on gadgets. One year, he decided to invest instead. Watching his portfolio grow gave him a sense of pride and control he never felt as a consumer.

Summary: Shifting from consumer to creator empowers you to build wealth and confidence. Maya and David discovered that creating value, rather than consuming it, transformed their financial lives.

5. Celebrating Progress, Not Perfection

The journey from scarcity to abundance isn't linear. It's filled with setbacks, challenges, and moments of doubt. The key is to focus on progress, not perfection. Celebrate each small step—whether it's saving $10, paying off a bill, or saying no to an unnecessary expense. These wins, however small, create momentum and motivation.

Perfectionism often leads to frustration and burnout. By embracing progress, you give yourself permission to be human and to learn along the way. This approach shifts your focus from what you lack to what you've achieved, cultivating a mindset of gratitude and abundance.

Examples:

1. Nina's Savings Journal: Nina tracked her progress in a journal, celebrating every milestone, no matter how small. Looking back, she realized how far she'd come, even when she felt she wasn't saving enough.

2. Carlos's Debt Journey: Carlos wanted to pay off $10,000 in debt but felt overwhelmed. He started with $1,000, celebrating each payment as a victory. This kept him motivated to continue.

Summary: Progress, not perfection, is the key to sustaining financial change. Nina and Carlos found that focusing on small wins kept them motivated and grateful for the journey.

6. Building a New Money Story

Your money story isn't just about numbers—it's about beliefs, experiences, and emotions tied to wealth. Changing this story requires rewriting the narrative you tell yourself about money. Shift from seeing yourself as someone who struggles to someone who thrives. Focus on abundance, gratitude, and empowerment.

This new story isn't about ignoring challenges—it's about approaching them with a new mindset. By embracing abundance, you create a financial identity rooted in confidence, purpose, and growth. This change doesn't happen overnight, but each step rewrites the script, turning financial struggles into a tale of resilience and triumph.

Examples:

1. Alicia's Gratitude Ritual: Alicia wrote down one thing she was grateful for about her finances every day, even if it was small. Over time, this practice rewrote her money story into one of abundance and gratitude.

2. Jordan's Generational Wealth Plan: Jordan grew up in poverty but decided to change the narrative for his family. By creating a savings and investment plan, he shifted his story from scarcity to building a legacy.

Summary: Changing your money story transforms your relationship with finances. Alicia and Jordan proved that reframing beliefs and actions can create a powerful legacy of abundance.

Chapter 10: " Automating Your Way to Wealth."

Chapter 10: Automating Your Way to Wealth

Part 1: The Power of "Out of Sight, Out of Mind" Savings

Automating your savings is one of the simplest yet most powerful tools for building wealth. By setting up an automatic transfer from your checking account to a savings account, you remove the temptation to spend that money. This "out of sight, out of mind" approach ensures consistent savings without the need for constant willpower. It's a psychological trick that transforms saving from a daunting chore into an effortless habit. Once you automate, your future self will thank you as those small, consistent deposits grow into a safety net or investment fund.

For example, let's say you automate $100 to transfer to a high-yield savings account every payday. Over a year, you'll have saved $2,400 without actively thinking about it. Add compound interest, and your savings will grow even faster. This strategy works because it eliminates decision fatigue, letting your money grow without interference.

Example 1:

Emma sets up her bank account to transfer $50 from each paycheck into her emergency fund. She forgets about it for a year and checks her balance to find $1,300, including interest. She's now ready for unexpected expenses like car repairs.

Example 2:

John automates $200 monthly into his retirement account. By the end of the year, he's contributed $2,400 and gained $100 in employer-matched contributions. His savings grow consistently, and he barely notices the money leaving his account.

Summary of Examples:

Automation removes the burden of decision-making and guarantees consistent savings, helping you achieve financial security effortlessly.

Part 2: Using Technology to Simplify Financial Growth

The digital age has provided tools that make managing finances easier than ever. Apps and online platforms allow you to track spending, monitor savings goals, and even invest effortlessly. Platforms like Acorns and Robinhood let you round up your purchases and invest the spare change, turning everyday transactions into opportunities for financial growth. Technology isn't just about convenience; it's a gateway to smarter, more efficient money management.

For instance, financial apps can categorize spending automatically, showing you where your money goes and where to cut back. Many apps also include features to set savings goals and notify you of your progress. These visual reminders keep you motivated and on track, ensuring that financial growth feels tangible and achievable.

Example 1:

Sarah uses an app to round up every purchase to the nearest dollar and invest the difference in ETFs. Over six months, her daily coffee habit of $4.25 contributes an additional $150 to her portfolio without her feeling the pinch.

Example 2:

Mike connects his budgeting app to all his accounts. The app alerts him when he overspends in his dining-out category and helps him adjust, saving him $200 monthly. He reinvests the savings into an IRA.

Summary of Examples:

Technology simplifies financial management, making it easier to save and invest without significant lifestyle changes or stress.

Part 3: Setting and Forgetting Your Way to Financial Success

The beauty of automation lies in its reliability. Once you set up recurring transfers or investments, there's no need to remember deadlines or worry about missing contributions. This "set and forget" method ensures that your financial goals are met without requiring constant attention. It's a way to overcome procrastination and build wealth effortlessly.

For example, setting up automatic payments to a debt repayment plan ensures that you stay on track to becoming debt-free without late fees or missed deadlines. Similarly, automating your retirement contributions ensures consistent growth in your nest egg while freeing your mental energy for other priorities.

Example 1:

Jake schedules automatic payments toward his student loans. By doing so, he avoids late fees and pays down his debt faster, shaving a year off his repayment plan and saving $500 in interest.

Example 2:

Lila automates 15% of her paycheck into her employer's 401(k) plan. Over five years, she accumulates $25,000 with minimal effort, benefiting from her employer's match and market growth.

Summary of Examples:

Automation ensures consistency and removes human error or procrastination, allowing financial success to unfold with minimal involvement.

Part 4: Automating to Overcome Emotional Spending

Automation removes the emotional element of spending, especially during periods of stress or impulse-buying urges. When your money is already allocated to savings or investments, it's harder to justify splurging on things you don't need. By automating your financial goals first, you reduce the temptation to spend on items that offer fleeting satisfaction but no long-term value.

Consider setting up direct debits for essential bills and savings before discretionary spending. This way, your financial priorities are handled, and whatever remains becomes guilt-free money for personal enjoyment.

Example 1:

Chris struggles with impulse purchases but automates $500 monthly into his Roth IRA before budgeting for fun. This method allows him to indulge in occasional treats without guilt, knowing his retirement is secure.

Example 2:

Maya creates an automated "fun fund" that caps her discretionary spending at $150 monthly. Once the account is empty, she stops spending, forcing her to stick to her budget.

Summary of Examples:

Automating key expenses and savings removes emotion-driven decisions, ensuring your money works for you before indulgences.

Part 5: Making the Most of Employer Benefits

Many employers offer benefits like 401(k) matching, automatic payroll savings, and Health Savings Accounts (HSAs). Taking full advantage of these automated options ensures you're not leaving free money on the table. Contributions are deducted before you even see your paycheck, making it easy to grow your savings without feeling the pinch.

For example, enrolling in an employer-matched retirement plan effectively doubles your investment. Additionally, HSAs provide a tax-free way to save for medical expenses while building long-term savings for healthcare in retirement.

Example 1:

Derek's employer offers a 4% match for his 401(k) contributions. By contributing $200 monthly, he gets an additional $200, doubling his retirement savings without extra effort.

Example 2:

Nina allocates $150 monthly to her HSA. Over two years, she saves $3,600, which covers medical expenses tax-free while earning interest.

Summary of Examples:

Employer benefits are powerful tools for automated wealth-building, offering additional growth opportunities without requiring extra income.

Part 6: Automating for Long-Term Financial Freedom

Automation allows you to focus on long-term goals while living in the present. By consistently saving, investing, and paying down debt, you create a financial foundation that grows steadily over time. This process transforms abstract goals into achievable milestones. The result is not just financial freedom but also peace of mind, knowing your money is working for you even when you're not actively managing it.

For instance, automating contributions to a diversified investment portfolio ensures you benefit from market growth over time.

Similarly, automating a debt avalanche or snowball plan keeps you on track to becoming debt-free faster, reducing financial stress and building confidence.

Example 1:

Rachel automates $300 monthly into a mutual fund. Over ten years, her consistent contributions and compounding growth turn into $50,000, enabling her to fund a dream vacation or early retirement.

Example 2:

Steve uses automation to focus on paying off his credit card debt. He schedules extra payments toward the highest-interest card, becoming debt-free two years earlier than expected and saving thousands in interest.

Summary of Examples:

Automation ensures steady progress toward long-term financial goals, reducing stress and providing clarity for the future.

Chapter Summary

Automating your financial processes creates a reliable, stress-free pathway to wealth-building. By leveraging tools and technology, automating savings, and taking advantage of employer benefits, you simplify your financial life and eliminate the risk of procrastination or emotional spending. Whether it's setting up small transfers or maximizing employer contributions, the key lesson is clear: consistent action leads to meaningful growth. Let automation be the silent force behind your financial success.

Chapter 11: " Celebrating Small Wins."

Chapter 11: Celebrating Small Wins

Part 1: The Psychology of Progress and Motivation

Celebrating small wins taps into the human need for recognition and achievement. Each milestone reached, no matter how minor, releases dopamine, the brain's "feel-good" chemical. This biological reaction reinforces the behavior that led to the win, encouraging consistent progress. For example, paying off a small debt creates a sense of accomplishment, motivating further action toward larger financial goals. Recognizing these moments not only boosts morale but also strengthens commitment to long-term objectives, making the journey feel rewarding.

Progress and motivation are intertwined. When you see results, even incremental ones, it breaks the monotony of routine and fosters hope. Small wins provide visible proof that your efforts are working. This psychological boost makes challenging goals seem achievable. Whether it's sticking to a budget for a month or saving your first $100 toward an emergency fund, acknowledging these achievements builds momentum for bigger changes.

Examples:

1. **Example 1:** Sarah decides to reduce her coffee shop visits and saves $30 in a month. She uses a portion of this to buy a specialty coffee blend for home, rewarding her success while staying within her goals. Lesson: Small adjustments yield results, and celebrating wisely reinforces good habits.

2. **Example 2:** Mike pays off his smallest credit card debt of $200. He writes it down on a "debt-free board" he keeps at home, visually marking progress. Lesson: Tangible reminders of success boost motivation and make abstract goals feel real.

Summary: Small wins keep motivation alive. Celebrating them shows that incremental progress matters and builds confidence for larger accomplishments.

Part 2: Rewarding Yourself Without Breaking the Bank

Rewards don't have to derail your financial goals. The key is aligning rewards with the scale of the milestone. By choosing meaningful, low-cost ways to celebrate, you maintain enthusiasm without undoing your progress. For instance, after completing a savings challenge, treating yourself to a picnic or a homemade gourmet meal can feel luxurious yet frugal. Celebrating doesn't mean splurging—it's about creating joy within your boundaries.

Strategically rewarding yourself ties success to positive reinforcement. By connecting a goal with a celebratory act, you form a mental association between effort and reward. This psychological link ensures you're eager to repeat the behavior. The reward should reflect the accomplishment's size; for example, finishing a budgeting month might warrant a small indulgence, while reaching a major savings milestone could justify a larger treat, like a modest weekend getaway.

Examples:

1. **Example 1:** Jenna saves $500 toward her vacation fund and celebrates by hosting a themed movie night with friends. Lesson: Thoughtful, low-cost rewards can offer joy and acknowledgment without financial strain.

2. **Example 2:** Jason tracks his expenses daily for 30 days and rewards himself with an inexpensive notebook for his next month's budget. Lesson: Small, practical rewards reinforce habits and provide satisfaction.

Summary: Rewards should inspire, not sabotage. Frugal celebrations create a balanced approach to staying motivated while maintaining financial discipline.

Part 3: How Little Milestones Lead to Big Changes

Small milestones act as building blocks for major transformations. Each time you achieve a minor goal, you're laying a foundation for the bigger picture. For example, consistently saving $50 weekly builds not only your savings account but also your confidence and financial discipline. These small actions compound over time, turning what once seemed insurmountable into achievable success.

Progress often feels intangible until small milestones make it visible. Tracking each step allows you to celebrate the journey, not just the destination. Whether it's paying off one bill or saving for a specific goal, these incremental wins serve as reminders of what's possible. Over time, they create a ripple effect, turning isolated actions into sustained behavior patterns.

Examples:

1. **Example 1:** Maria sets a goal to save $1,000 in six months by saving $40 each week. After two months, she's halfway there and feels encouraged to stick to her plan. Lesson: Breaking goals into smaller, achievable pieces builds momentum and keeps motivation high.

2. **Example 2:** Aaron wants to declutter his home but starts by organizing one drawer daily. A month later, his entire home feels lighter and more functional. Lesson: Small, consistent actions create significant results over time.

Summary: Small milestones are the seeds of larger success. Tracking and celebrating these steps builds confidence and creates lasting change.

Part 4: The Emotional Benefits of Acknowledging Wins

Acknowledging small wins is not just about motivation—it's also about emotional well-being. Celebrating achievements fosters gratitude, shifting the focus from what's lacking to what's already been accomplished. This gratitude reinforces a positive mindset, making you more resilient in the face of challenges. Feeling good about your progress creates a cycle of positivity that fuels further success.

Emotional rewards like pride and satisfaction are just as impactful as tangible ones. When you celebrate, you're giving yourself permission to feel joy and pride, which combats the negativity that can arise from focusing solely on what's left to achieve. This emotional recharge is essential for staying committed and excited about your goals.

Examples:

1. **Example 1:** Clara takes a moment to reflect on her first $1,000 in savings and writes a journal entry about how proud she feels. Lesson: Reflecting on achievements creates gratitude and reinforces a positive relationship with money.

2. **Example 2:** David creates a small photo collage of the experiences he's been able to enjoy by budgeting smarter. Lesson: Tangible reminders of success enhance emotional connection to progress.

Summary: Celebrating wins fosters gratitude and emotional resilience, keeping you energized and focused on future goals.

Part 5: Avoiding Perfectionism in Celebrations

Perfectionism often leads to the dismissal of small wins in pursuit of "bigger" goals. This mindset robs you of the joy of progress and makes long-term success feel out of reach. Embracing imperfection allows you to appreciate the incremental steps that contribute to the overall journey. For instance, saving $10 might not seem significant, but acknowledging it as a step toward financial freedom builds a positive habit.

It's essential to understand that no progress is too small to celebrate. Avoid the trap of thinking that only large milestones matter. Every effort you make, no matter how minor, is a victory against inertia and complacency. By celebrating these small actions, you create a more sustainable path to achieving your broader goals.

Examples:

1. **Example 1:** Kelly celebrates her ability to stick to a grocery list for the first time in weeks. Lesson: Recognizing even the smallest changes builds confidence and encourages consistency.

2. **Example 2:** Mark acknowledges his first successful day of tracking expenses and treats himself to a relaxing evening without guilt. Lesson: Even initial wins deserve recognition to reinforce new habits.

Summary: Rejecting perfectionism allows you to see and celebrate progress for what it is—proof that you're moving in the right direction.

Part 6: Building Momentum Through Small Wins

Every small win adds to a sense of momentum, creating a compounding effect. These victories serve as proof that you're capable of achieving what you set your mind to, fueling your confidence to tackle larger challenges. Momentum is the bridge between starting and succeeding, and celebrating along the way ensures you never lose sight of your progress.

Momentum creates a snowball effect—each win pushes you closer to your goals, making the next step easier. It's like climbing a mountain; each successful step builds the strength and determination to take the next one. Small celebrations along the way remind you why you started and keep you motivated to reach the summit.

Examples:

1. **Example 1:** Lisa tracks her spending for 10 days and uses her progress to commit to another 10 days. Lesson: Celebrating consistency builds confidence and encourages ongoing effort.

1. **Example 2:** Tom rewards himself with a relaxing weekend after sticking to his budget for an entire month. Lesson: Recognizing sustained effort fosters momentum toward longer-term goals.

Summary: Momentum is the result of consistent wins. By celebrating small steps, you ensure that progress feels rewarding and sustainable.

Conclusion:
Celebrating small wins is about more than just acknowledgment—it's about creating a positive cycle of motivation, gratitude, and progress. By recognizing incremental successes, you stay inspired, resilient, and aligned with your goals. These moments serve as proof that every step matters, paving the way for lasting change and ultimate achievement.

Chapter 12: " Investing in Yourself: The Best Return on Investment."

Chapter 12: Investing in Yourself: The Best Return on Investment

1. Spending on Skills, Education, and Personal Growth

Investing in yourself is the most powerful use of your money, yielding returns that compound throughout your lifetime. Skills, education, and personal growth are not expenses—they're assets that empower you to navigate life's challenges, seize opportunities, and create lasting value. Whether it's learning a new language, taking a professional certification course, or attending workshops that expand your skill set, these investments enhance your capabilities and confidence. When you choose to prioritize growth over fleeting luxuries, you're choosing to bet on your own potential.

The process of investing in personal growth also cultivates resilience and adaptability. In an ever-changing world, the ability to learn, unlearn, and relearn is invaluable. Spending money on coaching, therapy, or even self-help books equips you with the tools to manage stress, improve relationships, and set meaningful goals. These investments don't just change your circumstances—they transform how you see yourself and what you believe you're capable of achieving.

Examples:

1. Imagine a marketing professional who spends $500 on a digital marketing certification course. Within three months, they apply their new skills to their job, impressing their employer and securing a promotion with a $5,000 salary increase. The return on their investment is tenfold, and the certification continues to pay dividends in future opportunities.

2. A young entrepreneur invests $200 in a public speaking workshop. Initially nervous and self-conscious, they learn techniques to command an audience. Within six months, they use this skill to pitch their business to investors, securing $20,000 in funding that accelerates their growth.

Summary: In both examples, investing in personal growth directly improved earning potential and confidence. Skills and education are long-term investments that create opportunities far greater than the initial cost.

2. How Self-Improvement Transforms Your Earning Potential

Self-improvement is a powerful driver of financial success. When you actively work on becoming better—whether through learning new skills, improving your mindset, or enhancing your health—you position yourself to earn more and achieve more. Employers value employees who demonstrate initiative and are willing to adapt to evolving demands. Similarly, entrepreneurs who continuously upgrade their knowledge can better identify opportunities and outperform competitors.

Beyond tangible skills, personal growth also transforms your inner game. A confident, self-aware individual who invests in improving their communication, leadership, or organizational skills can achieve significant career advancement. By consistently working on yourself, you signal to the world—and to yourself—that you are capable of more, leading to new opportunities and increased earning potential.

Examples:

1. A sales representative spends $150 on an emotional intelligence course. The course helps them understand their clients' needs better and manage their emotions during negotiations. Over the next quarter, their sales numbers double, earning them a bonus of $3,000.

2. A software engineer takes up a $300 online course on machine learning. Six months later, they are recruited for a high-paying role in a tech startup, doubling their annual salary.

Summary: These examples illustrate how investing in self-improvement not only enhances tangible skills but also boosts confidence and performance, leading to greater financial rewards

3. The Link Between Knowledge and Wealth

The connection between knowledge and wealth is undeniable. Knowledge opens doors to opportunities that might otherwise remain closed. When you know more, you can do more, and when you can do more, you increase your earning power. Knowledge allows you to make better decisions—whether it's negotiating a raise, starting a business, or choosing investments. As you accumulate knowledge, you also accumulate leverage, positioning yourself as a resource that others are willing to pay for.

Wealth-building is not just about earning money but about knowing how to manage it. Financial literacy is a critical area of knowledge that transforms wealth into security and freedom. Spending time and resources to educate yourself on budgeting, investing, and money management can be the difference between a paycheck-to-paycheck lifestyle and financial independence.

Examples:

1. A young professional spends $50 on a personal finance book. They learn strategies to pay off debt and invest in low-cost index funds. Ten years later, their investments have grown into a six-figure portfolio, giving them financial freedom.

2. An aspiring investor attends a $300 real estate seminar. Equipped with practical knowledge, they buy their first rental property, which generates $500 in monthly passive income.

Summary: These examples demonstrate how knowledge translates directly into financial gains. The more you learn, the more you can earn and grow your wealth strategically.

4. Investing in Your Health as a Financial Strategy

Your health is your greatest asset. Without it, the ability to work, create, and earn is compromised. Investing in your physical and mental well-being—whether through gym memberships, healthy food, or stress management practices—is an investment in your productivity and longevity. When you're healthy, you have more energy, focus, and resilience, enabling you to perform better in every area of life.

Ignoring health often leads to costly consequences, from medical bills to lost income due to illness. Preventative measures, like regular exercise, balanced nutrition, and mindfulness practices, not only save money in the long term but also enhance your quality of life. A healthy body and mind are the foundation upon which financial success is built.

Examples:

1. A freelance writer invests $1,000 in ergonomic office equipment and a gym membership. Over a year, they experience fewer back problems, allowing them to take on more projects and increase their income by $10,000.

2. A high-stress executive starts therapy, spending $150 per session. Within a few months, they develop healthier coping mechanisms, leading to improved focus and a successful negotiation for a higher salary.

Summary: These examples show that prioritizing health pays off not just in physical and mental well-being but also in sustained and enhanced earning potential.

5. Building a Network Through Strategic Investment

Investing in relationships and networking can yield exponential returns. Attending conferences, joining professional organizations, or even paying for mentorship connects you with people who can open doors to new opportunities. The adage "It's not what you know, but who you know" often holds true—strategic relationships can lead to career advancements, collaborations, and partnerships.

Building a network isn't just about taking—it's about creating value for others. When you invest in relationships by showing up, offering support, and being genuine, you create a reputation that attracts opportunities. Strategic networking helps you tap into resources and knowledge you might not have on your own.

Examples:

1. A junior designer spends $500 to attend a design conference, where they meet a hiring manager from a top firm. Within three months, they secure a job that increases their salary by 30%.

1. 2. An entrepreneur invests $1,000 in a mentorship program with an industry leader. The mentor provides insights that help them scale their business, doubling revenue within a year.

Summary: Networking investments provide access to opportunities and knowledge that can accelerate success far beyond the cost of participation.

6. The Ripple Effect of Personal Investment

Every dollar spent on self-improvement creates a ripple effect that extends beyond financial gains. As you grow, you inspire others around you—your family, friends, and colleagues—to do the same. This ripple effect multiplies your impact, turning personal success into a shared journey. Investing in yourself sets an example for others, creating a legacy of growth and empowerment.

Moreover, personal investment increases your sense of self-worth. When you prioritize your growth, you send a message to yourself that you are valuable and capable. This shift in mindset enhances not only your financial outcomes but also your overall happiness and fulfillment.

Examples:
1. A parent spends $500 on a financial literacy course and starts budgeting effectively. Over time, their children observe and adopt similar habits, building their own savings early in life.

2. A teacher invests $200 in public speaking training and uses their newfound skills to inspire students, leading to a promotion to a leadership role.

Summary: The ripple effect of personal investment shows that the benefits extend beyond yourself, positively influencing others and creating a lasting impact.

Key Takeaway

Investing in yourself is the most profitable decision you can make. Whether it's through skills, health, relationships, or knowledge, the returns are far-reaching—enhancing your earning potential, quality of life, and impact on others.

Chapter 13: "Turning Expenses Into Opportunities."

Chapter 13: Turning Expenses Into Opportunities

Part 1: How to Maximize Cash-Back Rewards and Loyalty Programs

Every dollar you spend has the potential to give back, transforming your routine purchases into opportunities for financial growth. Cash-back credit cards and loyalty programs are tools that reward you for what you're already buying. Instead of merely spending money, you're essentially earning a rebate on your transactions. Imagine buying groceries or gas and receiving a percentage of your money back in cash, points, or discounts. Over time, these rewards can accumulate into meaningful savings or even cover unexpected expenses.

However, maximizing these benefits requires intentionality. You need to choose the right programs that align with your lifestyle and spending habits. For instance, a frequent traveler might benefit from airline loyalty points or travel-focused credit cards, while someone who spends heavily on groceries might focus on supermarket-specific cash-back options. The key is to ensure you're not overspending just to earn rewards, but rather optimizing the expenses you already incur.

- **Example 1:** Maria uses a cash-back credit card that offers 3% back on groceries. Over a year, her monthly grocery bill of $500 earns her $180 in cash-back rewards, which she deposits into her savings account.

- **Example 2:** James frequently travels for work and leverages an airline loyalty program. By booking flights with his affiliated credit card, he accumulates points that eventually cover a round-trip ticket to his dream destination.

Summary of Lessons Learned: Rewards programs can transform necessary expenses into financial benefits, but they require strategic use and alignment with your lifestyle to avoid unnecessary spending.

Part 2: Side Hustles That Make Your Spending Work for You

Your daily expenses often present untapped opportunities to generate income. By incorporating side hustles tied to your routine spending, you can turn outgoing money into incoming cash. For instance, driving for rideshare services like Uber or Lyft while running errands can earn money alongside your existing schedule. Similarly, renting out tools, vehicles, or even spare rooms can offset the cost of owning them.

The beauty of this approach lies in its synergy with your existing habits. Instead of drastically altering your life to make extra income, you integrate earning opportunities into what you already do. This mindset shift not only alleviates financial pressure but also enhances your financial creativity, inspiring you to view spending as a springboard for earning.99

- **Example 1:** Amanda uses her car for grocery shopping every week and signs up as a delivery driver for Instacart. By delivering groceries for others during her trips, she earns $200 a month.

- **Example 2:** Ryan, a tech enthusiast, rents out his high-end camera equipment when he's not using it. The additional $300 he earns monthly covers his camera's purchase cost within a year.

Summary of Lessons Learned: Side hustles aligned with routine activities or existing assets can transform everyday expenses into income opportunities, reducing the financial burden of ownership.

Part 3: Strategies for Turning Everyday Expenses Into Assets

It's possible to reframe expenses as investments when you approach them strategically. For example, purchasing high-quality, durable goods may seem costly upfront but saves money in the long run by reducing the frequency of replacements. Similarly, investing in education or skills training can lead to higher income, turning the cost into a return-generating asset.

Another approach is leveraging tax benefits associated with certain expenses. For example, homeowners can deduct mortgage interest, and freelancers can write off home office expenses. By understanding and utilizing these opportunities, you turn unavoidable costs into tools for financial gain.

- **Example 1:** Sarah opts to buy a more expensive but energy-efficient washing machine. Over three years, she saves $400 in utility bills, recouping the higher initial cost and reducing her carbon footprint.

- **Example 2:** Jonathan spends $1,500 on an online certification course for project management. Within six months, he secures a promotion that increases his annual salary by $10,000.

Summary of Lessons Learned: Strategic spending can transform unavoidable expenses into long-term assets, offering both financial and personal growth.

Part 4: The Psychology of Turning Expenses Into Opportunities

Reframing how you view expenses is as much about mindset as it is about strategy. Instead of seeing purchases as mere outflows of money, you begin to see them as investments in your future. This psychological shift fosters a proactive approach to finances, encouraging innovation and intentionality in spending decisions.

When you approach every expense with the question, How can this work for me? you open the door to financial creativity. By focusing on maximizing benefits and reducing waste, you not only save money but also empower yourself with a sense of control over your finances.

- **Example 1:** Ethan, a coffee lover, decides to invest in a high-quality coffee maker instead of buying $4 lattes daily. Over a year, he saves $1,000, while still enjoying his favorite beverage at home.

- **Example 2:** Lisa uses cashback earned on her household credit card to fund small family treats, turning what could be mundane spending into joyful experiences without extra cost.

Summary of Lessons Learned: A mindset shift toward seeing expenses as opportunities fosters creativity and empowerment, encouraging intentional and rewarding financial decisions.

Part 5: Overcoming Challenges in Optimizing Expenses

Implementing these strategies isn't always straightforward. You may face barriers like limited knowledge about rewards programs, upfront costs for durable goods, or the effort required to set up a side hustle. However, these challenges can be mitigated by breaking down actions into smaller, manageable steps.

For instance, researching the best cash-back card takes time but ensures alignment with your habits. Similarly, while a side hustle might require initial effort, integrating it with your routine makes it sustainable. Overcoming these obstacles is about persistence, planning, and focusing on long-term benefits.

- **Example 1:** Maya spends a weekend researching cash-back credit cards and switches to one that offers better rewards for her lifestyle. Within a month, she sees a noticeable improvement in her savings.
- **Example 2:** Tom spends time networking to rent out his unused truck. Though it takes effort initially, he eventually secures a steady income stream, covering his insurance and maintenance costs.

Summary of Lessons Learned: While turning expenses into opportunities requires initial effort, persistence and planning ensure long-term financial benefits that outweigh the challenges.

Part 6: Building a Habit of Seeing Opportunity

The real power of these strategies lies in making them habitual. As you practice looking for opportunities in every expense, it becomes second nature to approach finances creatively. Small wins build momentum, reinforcing the value of turning outflows into inflows.

Developing this habit requires consistent reflection and adaptation. Regularly reviewing your spending, identifying areas for improvement, and celebrating successes keeps you motivated and focused. Over time, you'll see every expense as a potential lever for financial growth.

- **Example 1:** Karen schedules monthly reviews of her expenses, looking for additional ways to maximize rewards or reduce unnecessary spending. Over a year, she saves $2,500 without feeling deprived.

- **Example 2:** Ben integrates his side hustle with his daily routine and tracks his earnings against expenses. Seeing measurable progress motivates him to explore new opportunities for growth.

Summary of Lessons Learned: Building a habit of seeking financial opportunity in expenses creates a powerful mindset that consistently transforms costs into growth, fostering long-term financial resilience.

Conclusion

Turning expenses into opportunities is a transformative approach that combines strategy, creativity, and persistence. Whether it's through cash-back rewards, side hustles, or strategic spending, the key takeaway is this: your money can work harder for you when approached with intentionality and purpose. By adopting these methods and maintaining a proactive mindset, you can transform your financial outlook and create a future of abundance.

Chapter 14: "The Debt Detox: Clearing the Path to Freedom."

Chapter 14: The Debt Detox: Clearing the Path to Freedom

Part 1: Breaking the Chains of Credit Card Dependency

Credit cards can feel like a double-edged sword: a symbol of freedom that often becomes a trap. The allure of immediate gratification tempts us to swipe now and worry later, but that "worry later" quickly snowballs into mounting debt. Breaking free from credit card dependency starts with understanding how it hooks you —through convenience, rewards, and the illusion of control. Recognizing this pattern empowers you to take the first step toward freedom: limiting your reliance on credit for everyday expenses.

Taking control means learning to pause before every swipe, questioning whether the purchase aligns with your financial goals or is just another impulse buy. By switching to cash or debit for discretionary spending, you regain a tangible sense of what you're spending. It's not about deprivation but about reclaiming ownership of your financial decisions.

Examples:

1. Impulse Spending: Sarah always paid for groceries and gas with her credit card to earn points. Over time, she began adding impulse purchases, thinking, I'll pay it off next month. Months later, she found herself with $2,500 in revolving debt and interest growing. By switching to a cash-only grocery budget, Sarah not only reduced unnecessary spending but also started paying off her balance.

2. The Minimum Payment Trap: Jason had $10,000 in credit card debt but only paid the minimum monthly amount of $200. At that rate, it would take him decades to pay off, with thousands lost to interest. By switching to a debt snowball strategy (paying off the smallest debts first while maintaining minimum payments on others), Jason regained momentum and reduced his total repayment time to five years.

What We Learned: Credit card dependency thrives on convenience and short-term thinking. Transitioning to cash or debit forces accountability and helps avoid the psychological pitfalls of easy access to credit.

Part 2: Strategies to Pay Down Debt Faster

The weight of debt can feel suffocating, but paying it down faster starts with a solid plan. Two popular methods—the snowball and avalanche approaches—can help you build momentum and see progress quickly. The snowball method focuses on paying off smaller debts first to create quick wins, boosting confidence and motivation. The avalanche method, on the other hand, prioritizes high-interest debts, saving you money in the long run. The key is to choose a method that works for your personality and financial situation and stick to it consistently.

Automation also plays a critical role in faster debt repayment. Setting up automatic payments ensures you never miss a due date, avoiding late fees and additional interest. Allocating windfalls—like tax refunds, bonuses, or gifts—toward debt instead of discretionary spending can significantly accelerate your journey to financial freedom.

Examples:

1. Snowball Success: Emily had five debts, ranging from $500 to $5,000. By using the snowball method, she focused on paying off the $500 balance first, which she cleared in two months. Motivated by her progress, she tackled the next smallest balance, building momentum until all her debts were gone in three years.

2. Avalanche Advantage: Mark had a $15,000 credit card debt with a 20% interest rate and a $5,000 car loan at 5%. By prioritizing his high-interest credit card using the avalanche method, Mark saved over $3,000 in interest while simultaneously paying off his car loan within the same timeframe.

What We Learned: The right debt repayment strategy depends on individual preferences. Snowball builds confidence with quick wins, while avalanche minimizes interest costs. Both require consistency and dedication.

Part 3: The Emotional Weight of Debt and How to Overcome It

Debt isn't just a financial burden—it's an emotional one. The constant worry, shame, and stress it causes can spill into every aspect of life, affecting relationships, health, and self-esteem. Overcoming the emotional weight of debt requires acknowledging these feelings instead of suppressing them. Sharing your struggles with trusted friends or a financial coach can help break the isolation and provide the support needed to face your debt head-on.

One of the most powerful tools to combat debt-induced anxiety is visualization. Imagine the relief you'll feel when you're debt-free: waking up without dread, knowing your money is working for you instead of against you. Creating a visual representation, like a debt payoff tracker or vision board, turns that relief into a tangible goal, keeping you motivated during tough times.

Examples:

1. Isolation to Support: Mia felt ashamed of her $20,000 student loan debt and avoided discussing it with her family. After opening up to her sister, she discovered they could split expenses like rent to free up more money for her loan payments. With her sister's encouragement, Mia paid off her loan three years earlier than expected.

2. Visualization Success: Paul created a debt-free vision board with images of a paid-off credit card statement, a vacation he'd take once debt-free, and his dream home. Every time he felt discouraged, he looked at his board and refocused on his goal, paying off $25,000 in credit card debt in four years.

What We Learned: Debt is an emotional and financial burden. Addressing feelings of shame and using visualization techniques can provide relief and motivation to stay on track.

Part 4: Overcoming the Debt Mindset

The debt mindset convinces you that owing money is "normal" or that you'll never escape it, but this belief keeps you trapped. Shifting your perspective from debt acceptance to debt rejection is critical. Start by rethinking how you view money—not as a tool to get what you want now but as a resource to build the life you desire.

Debt often thrives on avoidance. The first step to overcoming it is confronting the numbers—how much you owe, to whom, and at what interest rates. By facing your debt head-on, you strip it of its power, taking back control of your finances and your mindset.

Examples:

1. Debt Is Normal Mentality: Marcus used to believe carrying credit card debt was just a part of life. After attending a financial literacy workshop, he realized this mindset kept him from pursuing wealth-building goals. He stopped using credit cards entirely and focused on paying down $30,000 in debt within five years.

2. Confronting Avoidance: Tina hadn't checked her credit card statements in months out of fear. After finally calculating her total debt of $12,000, she created a repayment plan and paid it off within two years.

What We Learned: Shifting your mindset from acceptance to control transforms how you approach debt. Confronting the reality of your situation is the first step toward freedom.

Part 5: Building a Debt-Free Lifestyle

Becoming debt-free isn't the end—it's the beginning of a new financial chapter. To stay debt-free, create habits that align with your goals. Focus on living below your means, building an emergency fund, and setting long-term savings goals. This approach ensures you're prepared for unexpected expenses without falling back into old patterns.

Debt-free living also involves redefining how you find joy. Instead of equating happiness with consumption, focus on experiences, relationships, and personal growth. A debt-free lifestyle isn't about restriction—it's about freedom to live on your terms.

Examples:

1. Emergency Fund Success: After paying off her debts, Lisa started saving $200 a month toward an emergency fund. When her car needed $1,500 in repairs, she covered it without stress, avoiding new debt.

2. Living Below Means: After becoming debt-free, Alan downsized his apartment and cut entertainment subscriptions, funneling the savings into an investment account. This allowed him to save for a down payment on a home within five years.

What We Learned: Debt-free living requires proactive habits and a focus on experiences and goals over material possessions.

Part 6: Celebrating the Journey to Freedom

Debt repayment is a marathon, not a sprint, and celebrating milestones keeps you motivated. Reward yourself at key moments—when you pay off a credit card, hit a savings target, or reduce your total balance by half. These celebrations remind you of your progress and help maintain momentum.

Reflecting on your journey helps reinforce the habits and mindset that led to your success. Take time to appreciate how far you've come, and use your story to inspire others to start their own path to financial freedom.

Examples:

1. Celebrating Milestones: When Jamal paid off his last credit card, he treated himself to a small weekend trip—paid for in cash—to celebrate his progress without jeopardizing his finances.

2. Inspiring Others: After becoming debt-free, Rachel started a blog documenting her journey. Her story inspired friends and family to take control of their own finances.

What We Learned: Celebrating milestones and reflecting on your journey reinforces positive habits and inspires others to pursue financial freedom.

Chapter 15: " Creating a Future-Proof Budget."

Chapter 15: Creating a Future-Proof Budget

Part 1: Adapting Your Budget to Life's Changes

Life is unpredictable, and your budget needs to be just as dynamic as the world around you. A rigid, unchanging budget might work for a short period, but what happens when unexpected expenses arise or your income changes? Adapting your budget ensures that it remains a living document, one that evolves with your life circumstances. For example, a sudden job loss or promotion requires re-evaluating priorities and reallocating resources. This adaptability prevents financial strain and keeps you prepared for the curveballs life throws your way.

Another critical aspect of adaptation is anticipating predictable changes, like seasonal expenses or upcoming milestones. From holiday spending to a child starting college, foreseeing these shifts allows you to adjust your spending and saving patterns accordingly. A future-proof budget is not just a tool—it's your financial safety net, evolving to support you no matter what changes life brings.

Example 1: A single professional gets a raise but instead of adjusting their budget, they succumb to lifestyle inflation—upgrading their car and dining out more frequently. By the end of the year, they've saved no more than they did before the raise. By revisiting their budget after the promotion and allocating the extra income toward savings and investments, they could have grown their wealth significantly.

Example 2: A couple expecting a baby plans ahead, increasing their healthcare and childcare budget months in advance. By cutting discretionary expenses and building an emergency fund, they avoid financial stress during this major life transition.

Summary of Learning: A flexible, adaptable budget acts as a financial compass, guiding you through both planned milestones and unexpected challenges. Anticipating changes and proactively adjusting spending can prevent unnecessary financial strain.

Part 2: Balancing Long-Term Goals With Present Needs

Creating a future-proof budget requires striking a delicate balance between your immediate needs and your long-term financial aspirations. It's tempting to prioritize the now—spending on entertainment, dining, or travel—at the expense of saving for retirement or paying down debt. However, failing to account for the future can lead to financial instability, even as you enjoy the present. A well-structured budget allocates resources to both timelines, ensuring that today's enjoyment doesn't jeopardize tomorrow's security.

Balancing these priorities requires identifying and categorizing your expenses. Label essential needs, like rent and groceries, while also designating funds for long-term goals, such as investing or saving for a home. This approach ensures that your immediate happiness is met without compromising your ability to achieve significant milestones. Financial balance creates peace of mind, allowing you to enjoy life now while building for the future.

Example 1: A recent graduate allocates their first paycheck entirely to discretionary spending, neglecting student loans. By the time repayment starts, they're overwhelmed by debt. A balanced budget would have included fun expenses while reserving a portion of their income for debt repayment and an emergency fund.

Example 2: A small business owner sets aside 20% of their monthly revenue for long-term investments, like expanding their business, while still budgeting for personal and operational costs. Over time, they achieve growth without sacrificing personal stability.

Summary of Learning: Balancing present enjoyment with future planning ensures financial health across all life stages. A budget that accounts for both timelines creates harmony between living well today and preparing for tomorrow.

Part 3: Staying Flexible Without Losing Focus

Financial plans can often go off track, but the key is maintaining focus while adapting to unforeseen circumstances. Flexibility doesn't mean abandoning your goals; it means recalibrating as needed. For instance, if an unexpected expense disrupts your savings plan, redirect funds temporarily but revisit your budget to get back on track. Staying flexible ensures that temporary setbacks don't derail your progress entirely.

Flexibility also means re-evaluating your financial goals as your priorities evolve. The dream of owning a luxury car at 25 might shift to prioritizing homeownership by 30. By regularly assessing your goals and aligning your budget with your current values, you maintain focus on what truly matters. Flexibility is not about compromise—it's about resilience.

Example 1: A freelancer faces a sudden drop in income during a slow season. Instead of abandoning their savings plan, they reduce discretionary spending and temporarily scale back on savings contributions. Once business picks up, they adjust their budget to restore the original savings rate.

Example 2: A family budgeting for an international vacation has to redirect those funds to cover unexpected medical bills. By staying flexible, they reallocate their budget and create a revised savings plan to still make the vacation possible the following year.

Summary of Learning: Flexibility in budgeting allows you to navigate life's unpredictability without losing sight of your financial goals. It's about adapting with grace while maintaining a clear focus on what matters most.

Part 4: Prioritizing Needs Over Wants

One of the biggest challenges in budgeting is distinguishing between needs and wants. Needs are essential—housing, food, and healthcare—while wants enhance your lifestyle but are not critical. Prioritizing needs ensures that the foundation of your financial stability is solid before allocating resources to less urgent desires. This disciplined approach prevents overspending on non-essentials at the expense of critical obligations.

However, it's important to allow room for enjoyment. A future-proof budget doesn't eliminate wants entirely but ensures they don't overshadow needs. By thoughtfully allocating a portion of your income for discretionary spending, you can indulge without guilt or financial strain.

Example 1: An individual decides to upgrade to a luxury phone plan while struggling to pay rent. By prioritizing housing and choosing a more affordable plan, they ensure their basic needs are met without sacrificing connectivity.

Example 2: A young professional creates a monthly "fun fund," limiting discretionary spending to 10% of their income. This approach helps them manage debt repayment while still enjoying occasional nights out.

Summary of Learning: Prioritizing needs over wants creates a solid financial foundation while leaving room for enjoyment. Striking this balance prevents unnecessary stress and promotes financial health.

Part 5: Building Buffers for Uncertainty

Life's uncertainties make financial buffers essential. An emergency fund, for instance, acts as a safety net for unexpected events like car repairs or medical expenses. Without a buffer, even minor disruptions can create significant stress and derail your budget. By consistently setting aside small amounts, you create a financial cushion that brings peace of mind.

Buffers also allow you to take calculated risks, like starting a side business or pursuing higher education. Knowing you have a safety net empowers you to make bold choices without the fear of financial ruin. A future-proof budget isn't just about managing the present; it's about preparing for the unknown.

Example 1: A single parent builds an emergency fund over six months. When their car unexpectedly breaks down, they cover the repair without relying on high-interest credit, maintaining financial stability.

Example 2: A recent retiree allocates part of their savings for potential healthcare costs. When a medical emergency arises, they handle it stress-free, knowing they planned for such scenarios.

Summary of Learning: Building buffers for uncertainty creates financial security and empowers you to navigate challenges confidently. It ensures stability and resilience in unpredictable situations.

Part 6: Automating and Tracking for Consistency

Consistency is the backbone of a future-proof budget, and automation can make this easier. Automating savings, bill payments, and debt repayments removes the risk of forgetting or overspending. It creates a seamless system that ensures your financial priorities are always met, even during busy or stressful times.

Tracking is equally crucial, allowing you to monitor progress and adjust as needed. Apps, spreadsheets, or even simple notebooks provide insights into spending patterns and help you identify areas for improvement. Automation and tracking work together to maintain financial discipline and accountability.

Example 1: A young couple automates their monthly savings and bill payments. This system ensures they never miss a due date or spend money earmarked for savings, helping them achieve their financial goals on time.

Example 2: A professional uses a budgeting app to track expenses. Over time, they notice recurring charges for an unused gym membership and cancel it, redirecting the money to their vacation fund.

Summary of Learning: Automation and tracking build consistency and accountability, making it easier to maintain financial discipline. These tools streamline budgeting and support long-term success.

Conclusion

Creating a future-proof budget involves flexibility, balance, and strategic planning. By adapting to life's changes, prioritizing needs over wants, and leveraging automation, you can build a resilient financial plan that secures both your present and future. Let me know if you'd like to refine or add more examples

Chapter 16: "The Emotional Rewards of Saving Smarter."

Chapter 16: The Emotional Rewards of Saving Smarter

Part 1: How Saving Translates to Freedom and Peace of Mind

Saving money isn't just about numbers on a balance sheet; it's about the deep emotional relief that comes from knowing you have a safety net. Imagine the peace of mind that washes over you when a car repair bill no longer sends you into a panic. Saving transforms financial chaos into clarity, providing a sense of security that allows you to focus on living rather than just surviving. When your savings grow, so does your confidence, as each dollar saved is a step closer to financial independence.

Beyond financial relief, saving also gives you the freedom to make life decisions without fear. You can pursue opportunities—whether it's starting a business, taking a dream vacation, or simply leaving a toxic job—without being tethered to financial insecurity. The emotional burden of living paycheck to paycheck is replaced with a lightness that allows you to dream, plan, and act with purpose. Saving is not deprivation; it's empowerment.

Examples:

1. Lisa, a single mother, created an emergency fund over six months by cutting back on dining out. When her car broke down unexpectedly, the repair cost of $800 didn't cause stress. Instead, she paid for it immediately, feeling proud and secure.

2. Michael, a young professional, saved enough to take a six-month sabbatical to travel and reset his career goals. The freedom to pause and reassess his life without financial strain brought him immense peace and clarity.

Summary:

Both examples show how saving fosters freedom and peace of mind. Lisa's emergency fund protected her from stress during an unexpected event, while Michael's savings allowed him to explore personal growth without fear of financial instability.

Part 2: Rediscovering Joy in Simplicity

In a world driven by consumerism, saving allows you to rediscover the joy in simplicity. When you stop chasing every new gadget or trend, you realize that happiness doesn't come from things but from experiences and connections. Saving encourages you to focus on what truly matters—time with family, personal growth, or enjoying nature. This shift from materialism to simplicity brings a sense of fulfillment that possessions can't provide.

Simplicity also creates space for gratitude. When you stop filling your life with unnecessary purchases, you start appreciating what you already have. This newfound perspective helps you align your spending with your values, allowing you to savor small joys like a heartfelt conversation or a walk in the park. Saving isn't about denying yourself; it's about embracing a richer, more intentional life.

Examples:

1. Amanda downsized her wardrobe to focus on versatile, high-quality pieces. She realized she didn't need dozens of shoes to feel fashionable and began appreciating the simplicity of owning only what she truly loved.
1. 2. James started hosting potluck dinners instead of dining at expensive restaurants. These gatherings brought him closer to his friends and reminded him that meaningful connections, not pricey meals, bring happiness.

Summary:

Both examples highlight the joy of simplicity. Amanda found happiness in a minimalist wardrobe, while James discovered deeper connections through affordable social activities. In both cases, saving money enhanced their lives by focusing on what truly mattered.

Part 3: The Confidence That Comes From Financial Control

Taking control of your finances builds a quiet yet powerful confidence. Each time you save, you're proving to yourself that you have the discipline and foresight to prioritize your future. This sense of accomplishment translates into other areas of your life, reinforcing your belief in your ability to tackle challenges and achieve goals. Financial control isn't just practical—it's deeply empowering.

Confidence also grows when you realize that you're no longer at the mercy of external factors like an economic downturn or an unexpected expense. With a robust savings account, you feel prepared for the unexpected. This preparedness turns fear into self-assurance, as you know you've built a financial foundation that can weather storms.

Examples:

1. Sarah, who previously struggled with impulsive spending, began tracking her expenses and setting monthly savings goals. Seeing her savings grow gave her a sense of pride and control that boosted her overall self-esteem.

2. Carlos paid off his credit card debt and started saving 20% of his income. The knowledge that he was financially stable allowed him to confidently negotiate a better position at his job without fear of losing his income.

Summary:

Both Sarah and Carlos gained confidence from financial control. Sarah's discipline improved her self-esteem, while Carlos's financial stability empowered him to take career risks. Saving is not just about money—it's about reclaiming your power.

Part 4: How Saving Builds Emotional Resilience

Savings act as an emotional buffer, providing stability in life's unpredictable moments. When you know you have financial resources to fall back on, you can face challenges with a clearer mind and less anxiety. This emotional resilience helps you make better decisions under pressure, as you're not operating from a place of fear.

Beyond stability, saving strengthens your sense of self-reliance. It's a reminder that you're capable of protecting and providing for yourself, even in difficult circumstances. This resilience builds over time, creating a cycle where emotional strength fuels financial discipline, and financial discipline reinforces emotional well-being.

Examples:

1. Emma lost her job during an economic downturn but had six months of living expenses saved. Instead of panicking, she used the time to find a new job that aligned with her long-term career goals.

2. Joshua faced an unexpected medical expense but avoided debt thanks to his savings. The experience left him feeling prepared and proud of his financial foresight.

Summary:
Both examples demonstrate how saving builds resilience. Emma's emergency fund allowed her to navigate job loss with composure, while Joshua's preparedness turned a potentially stressful situation into a moment of pride and relief.

Part 5: Saving as an Act of Self-Care

Saving is one of the most profound acts of self-care. It's a way of prioritizing your future needs and well-being over temporary wants. Every dollar saved is a message to yourself that you are worth protecting and investing in. This mindset shift transforms saving from a chore into a deeply personal expression of love for yourself and your future.

Moreover, saving reduces the stress that comes from financial uncertainty. Knowing you have a cushion allows you to focus on other areas of self-care, like physical health or emotional wellness. By creating a sense of financial security, saving gives you the freedom to nurture other aspects of your life.

Examples:

1. Rachel, who once lived paycheck to paycheck, started a savings plan to cover six months of expenses. The security she gained allowed her to focus on improving her mental health and exploring hobbies she had neglected.

2. Mark set up automatic savings for a vacation fund, allowing himself to enjoy guilt-free travel once a year. The act of saving made the trips even more rewarding, knowing they were part of his self-care strategy.

Summary:
Both Rachel and Mark show how saving serves as self-care. Rachel's financial security supported her mental health, while Mark's intentional saving enhanced his enjoyment of life's pleasures. Saving isn't just practical—it's an investment in your overall well-being.

Part 6: Saving as a Legacy for Future Generations
Saving doesn't just impact your life—it shapes the lives of those who come after you. By building wealth, you create opportunities for your family to thrive, breaking cycles of financial struggle. This legacy of savings is more than just money; it's a gift of freedom, choice, and empowerment for future generations.

Teaching children or younger family members the value of saving ensures that your financial habits extend beyond your lifetime. By modeling financial responsibility, you inspire those around you to adopt the same mindset, creating a ripple effect of empowerment and security.

Examples:

1. Vanessa started a college savings fund for her children, relieving them of future student debt. Her efforts gave them the freedom to pursue their dreams without financial burden.

2. James invested in property using his savings, creating generational wealth for his family. His children inherited both the property and the mindset of financial discipline.

Summary:
Vanessa and James exemplify how saving creates a lasting legacy. Vanessa's savings freed her children from debt, while James's investments secured his family's future. Saving is an act of generosity that transcends your lifetime.

Conclusion

Saving smarter is not just a financial strategy—it's a life-transforming practice. From providing peace of mind and fostering joy in simplicity to building confidence, resilience, and a lasting legacy, saving empowers you emotionally, mentally, and practically. The rewards go beyond the numbers, shaping a life of freedom, fulfillment, and purpose.

Chapter 17: " From Consumer to Creator: Redefining Success."

Chapter 17: From Consumer to Creator: Redefining Success

Part 1: Breaking Free From the Consumer Mindset

The consumer mindset is deeply ingrained in many of us, driven by a culture that equates possessions with happiness. We are bombarded daily with advertisements promising fulfillment through the latest gadgets, clothes, or experiences. This relentless cycle conditions us to believe that our worth is tied to what we own rather than who we are. Breaking free from this mindset requires a shift in perspective, moving from seeking validation through consumption to finding contentment in self-created value. It's about realizing that happiness doesn't come from external purchases but from internal growth and meaningful contributions.

Reframing consumption starts with identifying your motivations. Are you buying to fill a void, keep up appearances, or cope with stress? Once you recognize these patterns, you can replace them with healthier alternatives. Instead of scrolling through online shops, invest your energy in creating something—whether it's a skill, a hobby, or a long-term project. By focusing on what you can produce rather than consume, you redefine success as something intrinsic and lasting rather than fleeting and external.

Examples:

1. A woman who frequently shopped for high-end fashion to boost her confidence realized that her self-esteem didn't come from her wardrobe but from her professional growth. She redirected her spending toward career development courses and found greater satisfaction and stability.

2. A man addicted to buying the latest tech decided to focus on building his dream garden. The time spent nurturing plants replaced his desire for gadgets, giving him pride and peace in his accomplishments.

Summary: Both examples illustrate that shifting from consumption to creation can lead to deeper satisfaction. When you invest in personal growth or meaningful pursuits, you escape the hollow rewards of consumerism and build something truly valuable.

Part 2: Investing in What Matters Most: Your Future

True wealth comes from investing in what holds long-term value. This means putting your time, energy, and money into assets that grow or improve your quality of life rather than depreciate. Whether it's financial investments like retirement accounts, educational opportunities, or health and wellness, every dollar spent on your future creates a foundation for lasting success. By prioritizing these areas, you move away from short-term gratification and toward sustained fulfillment.

The emotional reward of investing in your future is profound. Each contribution to your savings, education, or well-being is a step closer to security and independence. Imagine the peace of knowing you can weather unexpected financial storms, seize life-changing opportunities, or enjoy retirement without stress. These investments not only safeguard your future but also reinforce your self-worth, proving to yourself that you value long-term stability over temporary pleasures.

Examples:

1. A young couple decided to reduce dining out expenses and used the savings to start an emergency fund. Within a year, they had enough to cover three months of living expenses, which provided immense relief when one of them faced a sudden job loss.

2. An entrepreneur who once splurged on luxury cars redirected her funds toward building a passive income portfolio. Years later, the dividends from her investments allowed her to retire early and pursue philanthropic passions.

Summary: The examples highlight how prioritizing the future over momentary indulgences creates resilience and opportunities.

Strategic investments empower you to face challenges and embrace your goals with confidence.

Part 3: Building a Life You Love Without Overspending

Creating a life you love doesn't require endless spending—it demands clarity about what truly matters to you. It's about aligning your actions and finances with your passions and values. This could mean downsizing to afford travel, prioritizing relationships over material goods, or spending on experiences rather than possessions. When you focus on your unique priorities, you realize that a fulfilling life isn't about how much you own but how deeply you live.

Living within your means doesn't mean depriving yourself; it means finding creative ways to enjoy life without financial strain. By budgeting thoughtfully and exploring affordable alternatives, you can create a lifestyle that balances joy with responsibility. Imagine hosting potluck dinners with friends instead of expensive outings or exploring nature instead of shopping malls. These choices foster meaningful connections and memories that far outweigh fleeting satisfaction.

Examples:

1. A family who felt burdened by a large home sold it and moved into a smaller, cozy house. The lower mortgage allowed them to travel frequently, creating cherished memories together.

2. A college graduate chose to rent a modest apartment instead of an upscale one and used the savings to fund trips to explore different cities. These experiences enriched her life far more than high rent ever could.

Summary: Both examples demonstrate that mindful choices and intentional living lead to greater happiness. By focusing on what you truly value, you can design a fulfilling life that doesn't compromise your financial health.

Part 4: Cultivating a Creative Mindset

When you transition from consumer to creator, your mindset transforms. You begin to see opportunities in challenges and solutions in scarcity. Instead of spending to feel accomplished, you find joy in building, learning, and contributing. Whether it's writing, crafting, cooking, or teaching, creation offers a sense of fulfillment that no purchase can replicate.

Creativity also nurtures resilience. By focusing on what you can make or improve, you develop a proactive attitude toward life. You start to rely less on external rewards and more on your ability to create your own success. This shift not only saves money but also enriches your sense of purpose and identity.

Examples:

1. A former shopaholic started a blog to document her journey to minimalism. The process of writing helped her reflect, connect with others, and turn her story into a source of income.

2. A retiree who once spent excessively on luxury hobbies found satisfaction in teaching woodworking classes. Sharing his passion not only fulfilled him but also provided extra income.

Summary: Creativity replaces consumption as a source of happiness and pride. When you create, you gain confidence, independence, and a sense of accomplishment that no purchase can provide.

Part 5: Overcoming Emotional Spending

Emotional spending often stems from stress, boredom, or the desire to impress others. Tackling this requires addressing the root cause rather than just the behavior. By understanding your triggers, you can replace impulsive spending with healthier coping mechanisms, such as journaling, exercising, or connecting with loved ones.

Developing emotional intelligence around money means recognizing the difference between needs and wants. It's about pausing to ask yourself, Will this purchase truly serve me in the long run? By aligning your emotions with your goals, you regain control over your financial choices.

Examples:

1. A man who often shopped online after stressful workdays began replacing this habit with evening runs. The exercise helped him release tension, and he saved hundreds of dollars each month.

2. A woman who felt compelled to buy gifts to maintain friendships started hosting game nights instead. The laughter and connection far outweighed the satisfaction of expensive presents.

Summary: Emotional spending can be replaced with healthier habits that align with your values. Addressing the "why" behind spending leads to stronger self-control and greater emotional well-being.

Part 6: Redefining Success

Success is often measured by wealth and possessions, but true success is about freedom, fulfillment, and impact. Redefining success means shifting your focus from what you own to who you are and the life you build. It's about living authentically, aligning your actions with your values, and using your resources to create meaning and joy.

By letting go of society's definition of success, you gain the freedom to define it for yourself. Whether it's financial independence, creative pursuits, or strong relationships, success becomes personal and deeply rewarding. This redefinition allows you to break free from external pressures and embrace a life that truly feels like your own.

Examples:

1. An executive downsized her career to spend more time with her children. Though her salary decreased, she found greater happiness and balance in her life.

2. A musician rejected fame and instead focused on teaching music to underprivileged children. The impact she made brought her more fulfillment than any accolade.

Summary: True success lies in living authentically and intentionally. By redefining what success means to you, you create a life that is rich in purpose and joy.

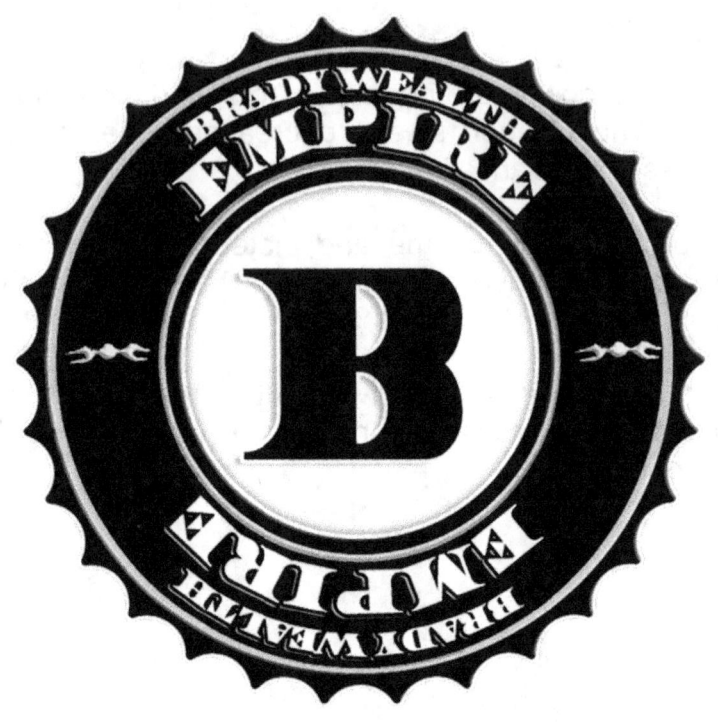

Chapter 18: " Empowering Others: Sharing the Wealth Mindset."

Chapter 18: Empowering Others: Sharing the Wealth Mindset

Part 1: How Your Financial Journey Inspires Those Around You

Your financial transformation is more than a personal achievement—it's a beacon of possibility for those around you. People notice the changes you make, whether it's your newfound confidence, the stability you exude, or the tangible milestones you achieve. These shifts spark curiosity. When others see you thriving without financial stress, they're inspired to ask questions and examine their own habits. By embodying financial freedom, you become a living example that change is possible, even in the face of challenges.

Inspiration is powerful because it bypasses resistance. Rather than lecturing or pressuring others to adopt better money habits, your actions speak louder than words. When someone sees you effortlessly paying down debt or celebrating a well-earned vacation funded entirely by savings, it makes the abstract idea of financial health feel attainable. Inspiration creates the first spark that leads others to believe they too can achieve the same.

Examples:

1. Role Model Effect: A friend notices you've started budgeting and cutting back on non-essential spending. After seeing how you've managed to save enough for an emergency fund, they start asking for advice on setting up their own budget. They begin tracking their expenses and find they can save an extra $200 a month.

2. Workplace Influence: A coworker overhears you talking about paying off a credit card early by using the debt snowball method. Inspired, they research it, apply the strategy, and begin paying down their debt aggressively.

Summary: These examples show how your journey can inspire others to take the first step. Your visible success acts as a catalyst, proving that financial improvement is achievable and worth pursuing.

Part 2: Teaching Family and Friends to Save Smarter

Sharing your wealth mindset with family and friends begins with compassion and understanding. Not everyone is ready to tackle their finances head-on, and approaching the subject without judgment is crucial. Start by sharing simple strategies you've used, like meal planning, negotiating bills, or automating savings. These small, actionable tips are easier to adopt and create immediate wins, building confidence.

When teaching others, it's essential to tailor advice to their circumstances. A single parent might need tips on reducing childcare costs, while a recent graduate may benefit from advice on avoiding lifestyle inflation. Offering personalized insights based on your own experiences makes the conversation relatable and actionable. By framing your guidance as support rather than criticism, you foster trust and create an environment where others feel safe to learn.

Examples:

1. Practical Guidance: A sibling struggling with overspending shares their frustration. You show them how to set up a budget using a simple app. After a month, they report saving $300 by cutting back on takeout and shopping sprees.

1. 2. Collaborative Learning: A close friend wants to start saving for a vacation but doesn't know how. You suggest setting up a joint savings challenge where each of you contributes $50 weekly. The shared accountability keeps them motivated, and they reach their goal faster.

Summary: These examples illustrate the importance of tailoring advice and offering practical, relatable tips. Small wins build momentum, helping others feel empowered to make smarter financial decisions.

Part 3: Creating a Ripple Effect in Your Community

Your financial journey can extend beyond your immediate circle and impact your broader community. Sharing your story in local groups, on social media, or through workshops can inspire collective change. Communities often face shared financial challenges, and seeing someone overcome those struggles can foster a sense of hope and unity.

When you create a ripple effect, the knowledge spreads far beyond the people you directly interact with. For example, when you host a free budgeting workshop at a community center or post about financial literacy on social media, attendees or followers may share your ideas with their own networks. This ripple effect amplifies the impact, empowering even more people to take control of their finances.

Examples:

1. Community Workshop: You organize a free workshop at a library to teach budgeting basics. Ten people attend, and one participant shares what they learned with their coworkers. The group starts a workplace financial literacy club.

2. Social Media Influence: You post a video explaining how automating savings helped you reach your goals. A follower implements the same strategy, shares their success story online, and motivates others to try it.

Summary: These examples highlight how your actions can inspire collective progress. By sharing knowledge on a larger scale, you contribute to a culture of financial empowerment.

Part 4: Overcoming Resistance and Building Trust

Not everyone will be immediately receptive to financial advice, especially if they feel judged or overwhelmed. Building trust begins with listening and empathizing. Instead of imposing solutions, share your own struggles and the lessons you've learned. Vulnerability creates connection, showing others that financial transformation is a journey, not an instant fix.

Breaking through resistance also requires patience. Celebrate even the smallest steps someone takes, like creating a budget or setting up an automatic savings transfer. Positive reinforcement encourages continued effort and signals that change is possible, even if it happens gradually.

Examples:

1. Empathetic Support: A friend dismisses budgeting as "too restrictive." Instead of arguing, you share how you once felt the same but found that tracking spending actually gave you more freedom. This perspective shifts their mindset, and they decide to try it.

2. Celebrating Small Wins: A family member saves $50 after taking your advice to negotiate their phone bill. You congratulate them enthusiastically, encouraging them to apply the same tactic to other bills.

Summary: These examples demonstrate the power of empathy and positive reinforcement in overcoming resistance. Building trust creates a foundation for long-term financial growth.

Part 5: Sustaining the Ripple Effect Over Time

Empowering others is an ongoing process. As people in your circle begin to adopt better financial habits, they may encounter setbacks or lose motivation. Staying engaged by checking in periodically, sharing additional tips, or celebrating their milestones helps them stay on track. Your ongoing support ensures that the changes they make are sustainable.

Sustaining the ripple effect also means expanding your reach. As your confidence grows, you might consider mentoring others, creating content, or collaborating with organizations to promote financial literacy. By remaining an active advocate for financial empowerment, you continue to inspire and uplift others.

Examples:

1. Follow-Up Support: A friend you helped start a budget struggles to stick with it after a few months. You check in, offer encouragement, and suggest simplifying the process to make it less overwhelming.

2. Mentorship: A community member asks for guidance on saving for a home. Over several months, you mentor them, providing tools and motivation that lead to their successful down payment.

Summary: These examples show the importance of ongoing engagement and expanding your impact. Empowerment isn't a one-time effort—it's a sustained commitment to helping others thrive.

Part 6: The Transformative Power of Community Wealth

When individuals adopt a wealth mindset, the collective impact is transformative. Families can break cycles of debt, communities can support one another, and a culture of financial literacy can flourish. Empowering others isn't just about teaching tactics—it's about inspiring belief in a better future.

This transformation creates a positive feedback loop: as individuals improve their financial health, they inspire and support others, multiplying the impact. The result is a community where financial stability becomes the norm, paving the way for generational wealth and lasting empowerment.

Examples:

1. Generational Impact: A parent learns budgeting from your guidance and teaches their children to save early. Those children grow up with strong financial habits, breaking the cycle of paycheck-to-paycheck living.

2. Community Growth: After attending your workshop, a group of attendees collaborates to start a community savings group, pooling resources to help one another achieve financial goals.

Summary: These examples illustrate how empowering individuals leads to broader change. The ripple effect creates lasting benefits for families and communities, fostering a culture of financial stability and growth.

By sharing your wealth mindset with empathy, inspiration, and consistency, you can create profound and lasting change in the lives of others and the communities you care about.

Chapter 19: " Conclusion - Your New Financial Life."

Chapter 19: Conclusion - Your New Financial Life

Part 1: Reflecting on How Far You've Come

1. Reflection and Gratitude:

As you stand at the threshold of your new financial life, take a moment to reflect on your journey. Remember the sleepless nights worrying about money, the moments of doubt, and the fear of never getting ahead. Now compare that to where you are today—equipped with knowledge, empowered by your choices, and focused on your goals. Gratitude is a powerful force that turns every small victory into a reminder of your resilience and strength.

2. Recognizing Growth:

Growth isn't just about numbers in your savings account or how much debt you've paid off. It's also the internal transformation—the shift in mindset from scarcity to abundance. You've cultivated the discipline to say no, the courage to face your finances head-on, and the wisdom to prioritize what truly matters. Acknowledge this growth as a significant achievement and a source of confidence for the future.

Examples:

- **Example 1:** Reflect on a time you were drowning in credit card debt. You felt stuck, but you took the first step: facing the numbers. Now, you've paid off your debt and experience the peace of not owing anyone.

- **Example 2:** Recall how you used to buy things impulsively to keep up appearances. Today, you're more thoughtful, spending only on items that align with your values, which leaves you fulfilled rather than regretful.

Summary: The examples show how far you've come—from a place of fear and impulsiveness to a life of intention and control. They highlight the emotional and financial rewards of staying committed to the journey.

Part 2: Staying Motivated on the Path to Financial Freedom
1. Embracing the Journey:

Financial freedom isn't a one-time event—it's a continuous process of learning, adapting, and growing. Motivation will ebb and flow, but reconnecting with your "why" can help you push through moments of doubt. Remind yourself of the life you're building—one free from financial stress and full of possibilities. Motivation thrives when paired with a vision for the future.

2. Celebrating Milestones:

Stay motivated by acknowledging every milestone, no matter how small. Whether it's saving your first $1,000 or making an extra payment toward your mortgage, each step is progress. Celebrate in ways that align with your new financial values—perhaps a homemade dinner with friends instead of an expensive night out. Every celebration reinforces your commitment to the path ahead.

Examples:

- **Example 1:** You've built an emergency fund for the first time, which gives you a sense of security. To celebrate, you plan a low-cost picnic with loved ones.

- **Example 2:** After hitting your goal of paying off student loans, you treat yourself to a modest but meaningful purchase—like a watch that symbolizes your time and effort.

Summary: These examples illustrate how celebrating progress can fuel motivation and reinforce positive habits, showing that financial freedom is a journey worth enjoying along the way.

Part 3: A Life of Freedom, Fulfillment, and Purpose
1. Redefining Success:

Your financial journey has taught you that success isn't about owning the most or earning the highest salary—it's about freedom, fulfillment, and purpose. Freedom to choose how you spend your time, fulfillment from meaningful experiences, and purpose in living a life aligned with your values. This mindset shift is the ultimate reward of financial transformation.

2. Living Your Best Life:
    Imagine waking up every day without the burden of financial stress. You're no longer tied to a paycheck or fearful of unexpected expenses. Instead, you're free to focus on the things that matter most—relationships, passions, and personal growth. This is the life you've worked for—a life that feels abundant because it's rich in meaning.

Examples:

- **Example 1:** You've reached a point where you can afford to take a career break to pursue a lifelong dream, like writing a book or starting a business.

- **Example 2:** Financial stability allows you to contribute to causes you care about, whether it's donating to a charity or mentoring others in financial literacy.

Summary: These examples highlight how financial freedom empowers you to live authentically and prioritize what truly brings you joy and purpose.

Part 4: The Ripple Effect of Your Transformation
1. Inspiring Others:
    Your journey doesn't just impact you—it inspires those around you. When friends, family, or colleagues see the changes you've made, they begin to believe in their own potential. By sharing your story, you become a beacon of hope and a resource for others seeking financial clarity.

2. Building a Legacy:
    The habits and lessons you've learned can ripple through generations. Whether it's teaching your children about saving or contributing to your community, your financial success creates a

legacy that extends far beyond your bank account. You're not just changing your life—you're reshaping the lives of those who follow.

Examples:

- **Example 1:** A family member notices your disciplined approach to budgeting and asks for advice, leading them to take control of their own finances.

- **Example 2:** Your newfound financial security allows you to start a scholarship fund, empowering others to achieve their dreams.

Summary: The ripple effect demonstrates how individual financial success has the power to uplift others, fostering collective growth and inspiration.

Part 5: Gratitude and Humility in Success

1. Staying Grounded:

Even as you achieve financial freedom, it's essential to remain grounded. Gratitude keeps you humble and connected to the journey that brought you here. Remember the struggles you've overcome and the lessons you've learned, and use them to guide your future decisions.

2. Giving Back:

Financial freedom isn't just about what you gain—it's also about what you can give. Whether it's time, money, or wisdom, giving back amplifies the sense of purpose in your journey. Sharing your blessings enriches your life and strengthens your connection to the world around you.

Examples:

- **Example 1:** You volunteer to teach financial literacy workshops, helping others avoid the mistakes you once made.

- **Example 2:** You start a community fund to support local small businesses, creating opportunities for economic growth in your area.

Summary: These examples reinforce the importance of gratitude and giving back as vital components of financial freedom, ensuring success remains meaningful and impactful.

Part 6: The Road Ahead
1. Continuous Growth:
   Financial freedom isn't the end—it's the beginning of a new chapter. Keep learning, adapting, and striving for improvement. Set new goals and challenge yourself to grow in ways that align with your evolving priorities.

2. A Vision for the Future:
   Envision a life where your finances support your dreams rather than dictate your choices. Whether it's traveling the world, retiring early, or pursuing a passion, let your vision guide you. The road ahead is yours to shape, built on the foundation of all you've accomplished.

Examples:

- **Example 1:** You decide to learn about investing, turning your savings into long-term wealth.

- **Example 2:** You set a goal to retire early and dedicate your time to causes you're passionate about, like environmental advocacy.

Summary: The road ahead is a continuation of growth and possibility, reminding you that financial freedom is not a destination but an evolving journey toward your best life.

This expanded conclusion ties together the key themes of reflection, growth, and purpose, providing readers with practical examples and emotional resonance to inspire their continued journey. Let me know if you'd like to refine any sections!

www.ingramcontent.com/pod-product-compliance
Lightning Source LLC
Chambersburg PA
CBHW071557220526
45469CB00003B/1047